The Massachusetts Poets

In the small state of Massachusetts a remarkable assemblage of Poets have given this corner of America a distinctive and honoured place in poetical history. Poets of the calibre of Amy Lowell, John Greenleaf Whittier, James Russell Lowell and George Cabot Lodge are speckled amongst Winifred Virginia Jackson, Gamaliel Bradford, G.O. Warren, Hilda Conkling and many others to bring you a rich reward of poems.

Index Of Poems

HOME-BOUND by JOSEPH AUSLANDE

The moon is a wavering rim where one fish slips,
The water makes a quietness of sound;
Night is an anchoring of many ships
Home-bound.

There are strange tunnelers in the dark, and whirs
Of wings that die, and hairy spiders spin
The silence into nets, and tenanters
Move softly in.

I step on shadows riding through the grass,
And feel the night lean cool against my face;
And challenged by the sentinel of space,
I pass.

AMERICA THE BEAUTIFUL by KATHERINE LEE BATES

O beautiful for spacious skies,
For amber waves of grain,
For purple mountain majesties
Above the fruited plain!
America! America!
God shed His grace on thee
And crown thy good with brotherhood
From sea to shining sea!

O beautiful for pilgrim feet,
Those stern, impassioned stress
A thoroughfare for freedom beat
Across the wilderness!
America! America!
God mend thine every flaw,
Confirm thy soul in self-control,
Thy liberty in law!

O beautiful for heroes proved
In liberating strife
Who more than self their country loved,
And mercy more than life!
America! America!
May God thy gold refine,
Till all success be nobleness,
And every gain divine.

O beautiful for patriot dream
That sees beyond the years
Thine alabaster cities gleam

Undimmed by human tears!
America! America!
God shed His grace on thee
And crown thy good with brotherhood
From sea to shining sea!

YELLOW CLOVER by KATHERINE LEE BATES
Must I, who walk alone,
come on it still,
This Puck of plants
The wise would do away with,
The sunshine slants
To play with,
Our wee, gold-dusty flower, the yellow clover,
Which once in Parting for a time
That then seemed long,
Ere time for you was over,
We sealed our own?
Do you remember yet,
O Soul beyond the stars,
Beyond the uttermost dim bars
Of space,
Dear Soul, who found earth sweet,
Remember by love's grace,

In dreamy hushes of the heavenly song,
How suddenly we halted in our climb,
Lingering, reluctant, up that farthest hill,
Stooped for the blossoms closest to our feet,
And gave them as a token
Each to Each,
In lieu of speech,
In lieu of words too grievous to be spoken,
Those little, gypsy, wondering blossoms wet
With a strange dew of tears?

So it began,
This vagabond, unvalued yellow clover,
To be our tenderest language. All the years
It lent a new zest to the summer hours,
As each of us went scheming to surprise
The other with our homely, laureate flowers.
Sonnets and odes
Fringing our daily roads.
Can amaranth and asphodel
Bring merrier laughter to your eyes?
Oh, if the Blest, in their serene abodes,
Keep any wistful consciousness of earth,
Not grandeurs, but the childish ways of love,
Simplicities of mirth,
Must follow them above
With touches of vague homesickness that pass
Like shadows of swift birds across the grass.
Beneath some foreign arch of sky,
How many a time the rover
You or I,
For life oft sundered look from look,
And voice from voice, the transient dearth
Schooling my soul to brook
This distance that no messages may span,
Would chance
Upon our wilding by a lonely well,
Or drowsy watermill,
Or swaying to the chime of convent bell,
Or where the nightingales of old romance
With tragical contraltos fill
Dim solitudes of infinite desire;
And once I joyed to meet
Our peasant gadabout
A trespasser on trim, seigniorial seat,
Twinkling a saucy eye
As potentates paced by.

Our golden cord! our soft, pursuing flame
From friendship's altar fire!
How proudly we would pluck and tame

The dimpling clusters, mutinously gay!
How swiftly they were sent
Far, far away
On journeys wide,
By sea and continent,

Green miles and blue leagues over,
From each of us to each,
That so our hearts might reach,
And touch within the yellow clover,

Love's letter to be glad about
Like sunshine when it came!

My sorrow asks no healing; it is love;
Let love then make me brave
To bear the keen hurts of
This careless summertide,
Ay, of our own poor flower,
Changed with our fatal hour,
For all its sunshine vanished when you died;
Only white clover blossoms on your grave.

THE RETURNING by SYLVESTER BAXTER

We long for her, we yearn for her
Yes, ardently we yearn
For her return.
Recalling those beloved days
(Days intimate with ways
Of friends so near to us
And life so dear to us),
We yearn unspeakably for her return.

And come she must... Yet while we trust
We soon may see the passing of this agony
Which makes intrusive years still seem
A fearsome dream,
We know that when she comes
She really comes not back again.

She'll come in other guise
And under fairer skies
And yet to bitter pain!
That day she went away
Our homes with laughing youth were filled.
Where then was happiness
Is now distress,
The laughter stilled;
For when she left
Youth followed her
We stay bereft.

So all our golden joy
For what she brings
Must carry gray alloy:
The sorrow that she cannot lay,
The mysery that she cannot stay
While all the gladsome songs she sings
Must bear for undertones
Old sighs and echoed moans.

As they who go away
In flush of youth
May come quite worn and gray
And bringing naught but ruth
So, when the strife shall cease,
And when she comes at last,
When all the armies vast
Shall at her feet
Kneel down to greet
Thrice welcome Peace,
This world will be so changed
(So many dear ones dead,
So many friends estranged,
So many blessings fled,
So many wonted ways forever barred,
So many coming days forever marred)
That then
She truly comes not back again
She, the Peace we knew.

Yet how we long for her!
How ardently we yearn
For her return!

TWO MOODS FROM THE HILL by ERNEST BENSHIMOL
I.
YOUTH
I love to watch the world from here, for all
The numberless living portraits that are drawn
Upon the mind. Far over is the sea,
Fronting the sand, a few great yellow dunes,
A salt marsh stumbling after, rank and green,
With brackish gullies wandering in between,
All this from the hill.
And more: a clump of dwarfed and twisted cedars,
Sentinels over the marsh, and bright with the sun
A field of daises wandering in the wind
As though a hidden serpent glided through,
A broken wall, a new-plowed field, and then
The dusty road and the abodes of men
Surrounding the hill.
How small the enclosure is wherein there lives
Each phase and passion of life, the distant sail
Dips in the limpid bosom of the sea,
From that far place to where in state the turf
Raises a throne for me upon the hill,
Each little love and lust of a living thing
Can thus be compassed in a rainbow ring
And seen from the hill.

II.
AGE
Why did I build my cottage on a hill Facing the sea?

Why did I plan each terraced lawn to slope

Down to the deep blue billowy breast of hope,
Surging and sweeping,
laughing and leaping,
Tumbling its garments of foam upon the shore,
Rustling the sands that know my step no more,
I should have found a valley, deep and still,
To shelter me.

There flows the river, and it seems asleep
So far away,
Yet I remember whip of wave and roar
Of wind that rose and smote against the oar,
Smote and retreated,
Proud but defeated,
While I rejoiced and rowed into the brine,
Drawing on wet and heavy-straining line
The great cod quivering from the deep
As counterplay.

What is the solace of these hills and vales
That rise and fall?
What is there glorious in the greenwood glen,
Or twittering thrush or wing of darting wren?
Give me the gusty,
Raucous and rusty
Call of the sea gull in the echoing sky,
The wild shriek of the winds that cannot die,
Give me the life that follows the bending sails,
Or none at all!

A BANQUET, ONE MEMORY FROM SOCRATES by ERNEST BENSHIMOL
After the song the love, and after the love the play,
Flute girl and pretty boy blowing
Bubbles of sparkling
Wine into darkling
Beards of a former austerity, stern even now, but
Fast growing
Foolish, with less of a stately
Reserve that held them sedately.
Oh Zeus, what a sight! With the wine dripping off it,
The grin of an ass on a bald-pated prophet.

After the feast the night, and after the night the day,
Fool and philosopher stirring
With the day dawning,
Stretching and yawning,
While in each wine-throbbing, desolated brain is the
Wheeling and whirring
Of thousands of bats, that the slaking
Of throats will not hinder from aching,
No wine for the brow that is beating to bursting,
But water at morning is quench for the thirsting!

SONG by GEORGE CABOT LODGE

Out of one heart the birds and I together,
Earth hushed in twilight,
Low through the live-oaks hung heavy with silver,
Gemmed with the sky-light,
Under the great wet star
Shaking with light, we jar
Lute-voiced the silence with intervaled music.

While under the margined world the slow sun lingers,
Flaming earth's portal,
Over the lilac dusk spreads his great fingers
Earth is immortal!
While the frail beauty dies.
Dream in the dreamer's eyes,
All the good gladness turns praise for the singers.

Hark, 'tis the breath of life! Hush! and I need it;
Northern, gigantic,
Questing the silences, herding the sudden foam
Down the Atlantic;
Leaves from the autumn's store
Shrill at my desert door,
They and I out of one heart that is grieving.

THE WORLDS by MARTHA GILBERT DICKINSON BIANCHI

I saw an idler on a summer day
Piping with Iris by a dancing brook;
And all his world was rife with Pleasures gay,
And languid Follies smiled from every nook.

I saw an artist in a world of dreams,
His rainbow rising from his radiant task,
To throw its magic prism beams
O'er Fancy's changeful masque and counter-masque.

I saw Toil, stooping underneath a world
Whereon his foster-brothers lighter tread,
His skyward pinions ever closer furled
Before the grim necessity of bread!

I saw a sinner working hard to be
Worthy his death-wage from the mint of time;
I saw a sailor, unto whom the sea
Was hearth and hope and love and wedding-chime.

I saw a mother living in her child
I saw a saint among his fellow men
Brave soldiery before my eyes defiled
And solemn-hearted scholars. Sudden then

I cried: "The stars are no less neighborly
In their ethereal remoteness swung,
Than these near human orbits wherein we
Live out our lives and speak our chosen tongue!

"Love seek through all, less there be one
Least soul unlit within the night
And over all, the selfsame sun
Give each creation light!"

THE RIOT by GAMALIEL BRADFORD

You may think my life is quiet.
I find it full of change,
An ever-varied diet,
As piquant as 'tis strange.

Wild thoughts are always flying,
Like sparks across my brain,
Now flashing out, now dying,
To kindle soon again.

Fine fancies set me thrilling,
And subtle monsters creep
Before my sight unwilling:
They even haunt my sleep.

One broad, perpetual riot
Enfolds me night and day.
You think my life is quiet?
You don't know what you say.

HUNGER by GAMALIEL BRADFORD

I've been a hopeless sinner, but I understand a saint,
Their bend of weary knees and their contortions long and faint,
And the endless pricks of conscience, like a hundred thousand pins,
A real perpetual penance for imaginary sins.

I love to wander widely, but I understand a cell,
Where you tell and tell your beads because you've nothing else to tell,
Where the crimson joy of flesh, with all its wild fantastic tricks,
Is forgotten in the blinding glory of the crucifix.

I cannot speak for others, but my inmost soul is torn
With a battle of desires making all my life forlorn.
There are moments when I would untread the paths that I have trod.
I'm a haunter of the devil, but I hunger after God.

EXIT GOD by GAMALIEL BRADFORD

Of old our father's God was real,
Something they almost saw,
Which kept them to a stern ideal
And scourged them into awe.

They walked the narrow path of right

Most vigilantly well,
Because they feared eternal night
And boiling depths of Hell.

Now Hell has wholly boiled away
And God become a shade.
There is no place for him to stay
In all the world He made.

The followers of William James
Still let the Lord exist,
And call Him by imposing names,
A venerable list.
But nerve and muscle only count,
Gray matter of the brain,
And an astonishing amount
Of inconvenient pain.

I sometimes wish that God were back
In this dark world and wide;
For though sonic virtues He might lack,
He had his pleasant side.

ROUSSEAU by GAMALIEL BRADFORD
That odd, fantastic ass, Rousseau,
Declared himself unique.
How men persist in doing so,
Puzzles me more than Greek.

The sins that tarnish whore and thief
Beset me every day.
My most ethereal belief
Inhabits common clay.

JOHN MASEFIELD by AMY BRIDGEMAN
I
MASEFIELD (HIMSELF)
God said, and frowned, as He looked on Shropshire clay:
"Alone, 'twont do; composite, would I make
This man-child rare; 'twere well, methinks, to take
A handful from the Stratford tomb, and weigh
A few of Shelley's ashes; Bunyan may
Contribute, too, and, for my sweet Son's sake,
I'll visit Avalon; then, let me slake
The whole with Wyclif-water from the Bay.

A sailor, he! Too godly, though, I fear;
Offset it with tobacco! Next, I'll find
Hedge-roses, star-dust, and a vagrant's mind;
His mother's heart now let me breathe upon;
When west winds blow, I'll whisper in her ear:
"Apocalypse awaits him; call him John!"

II

HIS PORTRAIT

A Man of Sorrows! with such haunted eyes,
I trow, the Master looked across the lake,
Looked from the Judas-heart, so soon to make
Of Him the world's historic sacrifice;
Moreover, as I gaze, do more arise;
Great souls, great pallid ghosts of pain, who wake
And wander yet; all, weary men who brake
Their hearts; all hemlock-drunk, with growing wise:
Hudson adrift; Defoe; the Wandering Jew;
Tannhauser; Faust; Andrea; phantoms, all,
In Masefield's eyes you lodge; and to the wall
I turn you, hand a-tremble, lest you make
Of mine own stricken eyes a mirror, too.
Wherein the sad world's sadder for your sake.

III

HIS "DAUBER"

O Masefield's "Dauber!" You, who being dead,
Yet speak: heroic, dauntless, flaming soul,
Too suddenly snuffed out! Here take fresh toll
Of cognizance, and, in your ocean bed,
Serenely rest, assured that who has read
What you would fain have pictured of the Pole
Would gladly match your part against the whole
Of many a modern artist, Paris-bred.

And more than this: if you, indeed, are his,
Then, by a dual truth, he, too, is yours;
For, marked and credited by what endures,
Were it the only thing, which bears his name,
(O deathless Soul, I speak you true in this!)
"The Dauber" has brought Masefield to his fame.

IV

HIS "GALLIPOLI"

"Small wonder," speaks my pensive self, "that he
Whose passion 'tis to sing of men who fail,
(Belabored, broken by The Unseen Flail)
Small wonder that be makes Gallipoli

His fervent text, for could there be
A costlier failure in Earth's shuddering tale?
Think of heroic Sulva's bloody swale;
Of Anzac's tortured thirst and agony!"
But as I read, protesting voices cry: "Not we,
Not we, who fell among the daffodils,
Who conquered Death among those blistered hills,
And found our glory after mortal pain;
Not we, who failed and lost Gallipoli;
The sad, strange failure theirs who mourn in vain!"

V

HIS MEAD

So, Masefield, have your royal words once more
Called forth the praise of men, where praise is due;

Your great elegiac, tragically true,
Must leave all Britain prouder than before;
And, in spite of all that breaking hearts deplore,
And all that anguished consciences must rue,
One arrowed gladness surely pierces through
From London's centre to Canadian shore:

When England, sobbing, mourns Gallipoli,
When warm tears flow for Rupert Brooke
And all the splendid Youth her error took
As hostage from the fields of daffodils,
Let this a present, living solace be:
You are not sleeping in those cruel hills!

1620-1920 by LE BARON RUSSELL BRIGGS
Before him rolls the dark, relentless ocean;
Behind him stretch the cold and barren sands;
Wrapt in the mantle of his deep devotion
The Pilgrim kneels, and clasps his lifted hands;

"God of our fathers, who hast safely brought us
Through seas and sorrows, famine, fire, and sword;
Who, in Thy mercies manifold hast taught us
To trust in Thee, our leader and our Lord;

"God, who hast send Thy truth to shine before us,
A fiery pillar, beaconing on the sea;
God, who hast spread thy wings of mercy o'er us;
God, who hast set our children's children free,

"Freedom Thy new-born nation here shall cherish;
Grant us Thy covenant, changing, sure:
Earth shall decay; the firmament shall perish;
Freedom and Truth, immortal shall endure."

Face to the Indian arrows.
Face to the Prussian guns,
From then till now the Pilgrim's vow
Has held the Pilgrim's sons.

He braved the red man's ambush,
He loosed the black man's chain;
His spirit broke King George's yoke
And the battleships of Spain.

He crossed the seething ocean;
He dared the death-strewn track;
He charged in the hell of Saint Mihiel
And hurled the tyrant back.

For the voice of the lonely Pilgrim
Who knelt upon the strand
A people hears three hundred years
In the conscience of the land.

Daughter of Truth and mother of Courage,
Conscience, all hail!
Heart of New England, strength of the Pilgrims,
Thou shalt prevail.
Look how the empires rise and fall!
Athens robed in her learning and beauty,
Rome in her royal lust for power
Each has flourished for her little hour,
Risen and fallen and ceased to be.
What of her by the Western Sea,
Born and bred as the child of Duty,
Sternest of them all?
She it is and she alone
Who built on faith as her corner stone;
Of all the nations none but she
Knew that the truth shall make us free.
Daughter of Courage, mother of heros,
Freedom divine.
Light of New England, Star of the Pilgrim,
Still shalt thou shine.
Yet even as we in our pride rejoice,
Hark to the prophet's warning voice:
"The Pilgrim's thrift is vanished
And the Pilgrim's faith is dead,
And the Pilgrim's God is banished,
And Mammon reigns in his stead;
And work is damned as an evil,
And men and women cry,
In their restless haste, 'Let us spend and waste,
And live; for to-morrow we die.'

"And law is trampled under;
And the nations stand aghast,
As they hear the distant thunder
Of the storm that marches fast;
And we, whose ocean borders
Shut off the sound and the sight,
We will wait for marching orders;
The world has seen us fight;
We have earned our days of revel;
'On with the dance'! we cry.
It is pain to think; we will eat and drink!
And live; for to-morrow we die."

"We have laughed in the eyes of danger;
We have given our bravest and best;
We have succored the starving stranger;
Others shall heed the rest.'
And the revel never ceases;
And the nations hold their breath;
And our laughter peals, and the mad world reels,
To a carnival of death.

"Slaves of sloth and the senses,
Clippers of Freedom's wings,
Come back to the Pilgrim's Army
And fight for the King of Kings;

Come back to the Pilgrim's conscience;
Be born in the nation's birth;
And strive again as simple men
For the freedom of the earth.
Freedom a free-born nation still shall cherish,
Be this our covenant, unchanging, sure:
Earth shall decay; the firmament shall perish;
Freedom and Truth immortal shall endure."

Land of our fathers, when the tempest rages,
When the wide earth is racked with war and crime,
Founded forever on the Rock of Ages,
Beaten in vain by surging seas of time,

Even as the shallop on the breakers riding,
Even as the Pilgrim kneeling on the shore,
Firm in thy faith and fortitude abiding,
Hold thou thy children free forever more.

And when we sail as Pilgrims' sons and daughters
The spirit's Mayflower into seas unknown,
Driving across the waste of wintry waters
The voyage every soul shall make alone,

The Pilgrim's faith, the Pilgrim's courage grant us;
Still shines the truth that for the Pilgrim shone.
We are his seed; nor life nor death shall daunt us.
The port is Freedom! Pilgrim heart, sail on!

THE CROSS-CURRENT by ABBIE FARWELL BROWN
Through twelve stout generations
New England blood I boast;
The stubborn pastures bred them,
The grim, uncordial coast,

Sedate and proud old cities,
Loved well enough by me,
Then how should I be yearning
To scour the earth and sea.

Each of my Yankee forbears
Wed a New England mate:
They dwelt and did and died here,
Nor glimpsed a rosier fate.

My clan endured their kindred;
But foreigners they loathed,
And wandering folk, and minstrels,
And gypsies motley-clothed.

Then why do patches please me,
Fantastic, wild array?
Why have I vagrant fancies
For lads from far away.

My folk were godly Churchmen,
Or paced in Elders' weeds;
But all were grave and pious
And hated heathen creeds.

Then why are Thor and Wotan
To dread forces still?
Why does my heart go questing
For Pan beyond the hill?

My people clutched at freedom.
Though others' wills they chained,
But made the Law and kept it,
And Beauty, they restrained.

Then why am I a rebel
To laws of rule and square?
Why would I dream and dally,
Or, reckless, do and dare?

O righteous, solemn Grandsires,
O dames, correct and mild,
Who bred me of your virtues!
Whence comes this changing child?

The thirteenth generation,
Unlucky number this!
My grandma loved a Pirate,
And all my faults are his!

A gallant, ruffled rover,
With beauty-loving eye,
He swept Colonial waters
Of coarser, bloodier fry.

He waved his hat to danger,
At Law he shook his fist.
Ah, merrily he plundered,
He sang and fought and kissed!

Though none have found his treasure,
And none his part would take,
I bless that thirteenth lady
Who chose him for my sake!

CANDLEMAS by ALICE BROWN
O Hearken, all ye little weeds
That lie beneath the snow,
(So low, dear hearts, in poverty so low!)
The sun hath risen for royal deeds,
A valiant wind the vanguard leads;
Now quicken ye, lest unborn seeds
Before ye rise and blow.

O furry living things, adream
On winter's drowsy breast,
(How rest ye there, how softly, safely rest!)
Arise and follow where a gleam
Of wizard gold unbinds the stream,
And all the woodland windings seem
With sweet expectance blest.

My birds, come back! the hollow sky
Is weary for your note.
(Sweet-throat, come back! O liquid, mellow throat!)
Ere May's soft minions hereward fly,
Shame on ye, Laggards, to deny
The brooding breast, the sun-bright eye,
The tawny, shining coat!

SUNRISE ON MANSFIELD MOUNTAIN by ALICE BROWN
O swift forerunners, rosy with the race!
Spirits of dawn, divinely manifest
Behind your blushing banners in the sky,
Daring invaders of Night's tenting-ground,
How do ye strain on forward-bending foot,
Each to be first in heralding of joy!

With silence sandalled, so they weave their way,
And so they stand, with silence panoplied,
Chanting, through mystic symbollings of flame,
Their solemn invocation to the light.

O changeless guardians! O ye wizard first!
What strenuous philter feeds your potency.
That thus ye rest, in sweet wood-hardiness,
Ready to learn of all and utter naught?
What breath may move ye, or what breeze invite
To odorous hot lendings of the heart?
What wind-but all the winds are yet afar,
And e'en the little tricksy zephyr sprites,
That fleet before them, like their elfin locks,
Have lagged in sleep, nor stir nor waken yet
To pluck the robe of patient majesty.

Too still for dreaming, too divine for sleep,
So range the firs, the constant, fearless ones.
Warders of mountain secrets, there they wait,
Each with his cloak about him, breathless, calm.
And yet expectant, as who knows the dawn,

And all night thrills with memory and desire,
Searching in what has been for what shall be:

The marvel of the ne'er familiar day,
Sacred investiture of life renewed,
The chrism of dew, the coronal of flame.
Low in the valley lies the conquered rout

Of man's poor, trivial turmoil, lost and drowned
Under the mist, in gleaming rivers rolled,
Where oozy marsh contends with frothing main.
And rounding all, springs one full, ambient arch,
One great good limpid world, so still, so still!
For no sound echoes from its crystal curve
Save four clear notes, the song of that lone bird
Who, brave but trembling, tries his morning hymn,
And has no heart to finish, for the awe
And wonder of this pearling globe of dawn.

Light, light eternal! veiling-place of stars!
Light, the revealer of dread beauty's face!
Weaving whereof the hills are lambent clad!
Mighty libation to the Unknown God!
Cup whereat pine-trees slake their giant thirst
And little leaves drink sweet delirium!
Being and breath and potion! living soul
And all-informing heart of all that lives!
How can we magnify thine awful name
Save by its chanting: Light! and Light! and Light!
An exhalation from far sky retreats,
It grows in silence, as 'twere self-create,
Suffusing all the dusky web of night.
But one lone corner it invades not yet,
Where low above a black and rimy crag
Hangs the old moon, thin as a battered shield,
The holy, useless shield of long-past wars,
Dinted and frosty, on the crystal dark.
But lo! the east, let none forget the east,
Pathway ordained of old where He should tread.
Through some sweet magic common in the skies,
The rosy banners are with saffron tinct;
The saffron grows to gold, the gold is fire,
And led by silence more majestical
Than clash of conquering arms, He comes! He comes!
He holds His spear benignant, sceptrewise,
And strikes out flame from the adoring hills.

BURNT ARE THE PETALS OF LIFE by ELSIE PUMPELLY CABOT
Burnt are the petals of life as a rose fallen and crumbled to dust.
Blackened the heart of the past is, ashes that must
Forever be sifted, more precious than sunbeams that
open the budding to-morrow.
Once was a passion completed,-too perfect, the
Gods have not broken to borrow
Blackened the heart of the past is, ashes that must
Forever be sifted. O, loving to-morrow
The rose of the past is, Life-Eternity's dust.

FOUR FOUNTAINS AFTER RESPIGHI by JESSICA CARR
Fresh mists of Roman dawn;
For water search the cattle;

Faintly on damp air sounds the shepherd's horn
Above fountain Giulia's prattle.

Triton, joyous and loud
Of Naiads summons troops;
A frenziedly leaping and mingling crowd,
Dancing, pursuing groups.

At high noon the trumpets peal,
Neptune's chariot passes by;
Trains of sirens, tritons, Trevi's jets heal
Then trumpets' echoes sigh.

Tolling bell and sunset,
Twittering birds and calm;
Medici's fountain, shimmering net,
Into the night brings balm.

IN THE TROLLEY CAR by RUTH BALDWIN CHENERY

The swart Italian in the trolley car,
Hoarded his children in his arms and breast;
The mother, all unheeding, sat afar,
Her splendid eyes were vague, her lips compressed.

One Raphael-boy slipped from his father's knee,
Climbed to her side, and gently stroked her cheek,
She turned away, and would not hear his plea,
She turned away, and would not even speak.

With trembling lips the child crept back again
To the warm shelter of his father's breast;
We looked indignant pity, for till then
We thought that mother-love bore every test.

We rose to go, the father-mother said,
In deep, low tones, "Don't t'inka hard you bet
The younges' was too-seeck, and he is dead,
She will be alla right, when she forget."

When she forgets! "Great-Heart," hold closer yet
Thy precious brood and let it feel no lack!
Until her soul shall wake, but not forget,
When the warm tides of love come surging back.

IN IRISH RAIN by MARTHA HASKELL CLARK

The great world stretched its arms to me and held me to its breast,
They say I've song-birds in my throat, and give me of their best;
But sure, not all their gold can buy, can take me back again
To little Mag o' Monagan's a-singing in the rain.

The silver-slanting Irish rain, all warm and sweet that fills
The little brackened lowland pools, and drifts across the hills;
That turns the hill-grass cool and wet to dusty childish feet,

And hangs above the valley-roofs, filmed blue with burning peat.

And oh the kindly neighbor-folk that called the young ones in,
Down fragrant yellow-tapered paths that thread the prickly whin;
The hot, sweet smell of oaten-cake, the kettle purring soft,
The dear-remembered Irish speech, they call to me how oft!

They mind me just a slip o' girl in tattered kirtle blue,
But oh they loved me for myself, and not for what I do!
And never one but had a joy to pass the time of day
With little Mag o' Monagan's a-laughing down the way.

There's fifty roofs to shelter me where one was set before,
But make me free to that again, I'll not be wanting more,
But sure I know not tears nor gold can turn the years again
To little Mag o' Monagan's a-singing in the rain.

CRETONNE TROPICS by GRACE HAZARD
The cretonne in your willow chair
Shows through a zone of rosy air,
A tree of parrots, agate-eyed,
With blue-green crests and plumes of pride
And beaks most formidably curved.
I hear the river, silver-nerved,
To their shrill protests make reply,
And the palm forest stir and sigh.

Curious, the spell that colors cast,
Binding the fancy coweb-fast,
And you would smile if you could know
I like your cretonne parrots so!
But I have seen them sail toward night
Superbly homeward, the last light
Lifting them like a purple sea
Scorned and made use of arrogantly;
And I have heard them cry aloud
From out a tall palm's emerald cloud;
And I brought home a brilliant feather,
Lost like a flake of sunset weather.

Here in the north the sea is white
And mother-of-pearl in morning light,
Quite lovely, but there is a glare
That daunts me.
Now the willow chair
Suggests a more perplexing sea,
Till my heart aches with memory
And parrots dye the air around,
And I forget the pallid Sound.

TO HILDA OF HER ROSES by GRACE HAZARD CONKLING
Enough has been said about roses

To fill thirty thick volumes;
There are as many songs about roses
As there are roses in the world
That includes Mexico ... the Azores ... Oregon...

It is a pity your roses
Are too late for Omar...
It is a pity Keats has gone...

Yet there must be something left to say
Of flowers like these!
Adventurers,
They pushed their way
Through dewy tunnels of the June night
Now they confer....
A little tremulous....
Dazzled by the yellow sea-beach of morning

If Herrick would tiptoe back...
If Blake were to look this way
Ledwidge, even!

DANDELION by HILDA CONKLING

Little soldier with the golden helmet,
O What are you guarding on my lawn?
You with your green gun
And your yellow beard,
Why do you stand so stiff?
There is only the grass to fight!

RED ROOSTER by HILDA CONKLING

Red Rooster in your gray coop,
O stately creature with tail-feathers red and blue,
Yellow and black,
You have a comb gay as a parade
On your head:
You have pearl trinkets
On your feet:
The short feathers smooth along your back
Are the dark color of wet rocks,
Or the rippled green of ships
When I look at their sides through water.
I don't know how you happened to be made
So proud, so foolish,
Wearing your coat of many colors,
Shouting all day long your crooked words,
Loud... sharp... not beautiful!

VELVETS (BY A BED OF PANSIES) by HILDA CONKLING

This pansy has a thinking face
Like the yellow moon.

This one has a face with white blots;
I call him the clown.
Here goes one down the grass
With a pretty look of plumpness;
She is a little girl going to school
With her hands in the pockets of her pinafore.
Her name is Sue.
I like this one, in a bonnet,
Waiting,
Her eyes are so deep!
But these on the other side,
These that wear purple and blue,
They are the Velvets,
The king with his cloak,
The queen with her gown,
The prince with his feather.
These are dark and quiet
And stay alone.
I know you, Velvets,
Color of Dark,
Like the pine-tree on the hill
When stars shine!

THE MOODS by FANNIE STEARNS DAVIS

THE Moods have laid their hands across my hair:
The Moods have drawn their fingers through my heart;
My hair shall never more lie smooth and bright,
But stir like tide-worn sea-weed, and my heart
Shall never more be glad of small sweet things,
A wild rose, or a crescent moon,-a book
Of little verses, or a dancing child.
My heart turns crying from the rose and book,
My heart turns crying from the thin bright moon,
And weeps with useless sorrow for the child.
The Moods have loosed a wind to vex my hair,
And made my heart too wise, that was a child.

Now I shall blow like smitten candle-flame:
I shall desire all things that may not be:
The years, the stars, the souls of ancient men,
All tears that must, and smiles that may not be,
Yes, glimmering lights across a windy ford,
And vagrant voices on a darkened plain,
And holy things, and outcast things, and things,
Far too remote, frail-bodied to be plain.

My pity and my joy are grown alike.
I cannot sweep the strangeness from my heart.
The Moods have laid swift hands across my hair:
The Moods have drawn swift fingers through my heart.

HILL-FANTASY by FANNIE STEARNS DAVIS

Sitteth by the red cairn a brown One, a hoofed One,

High upon the mountain, where the grasses fail.
Where the ash-trees flourish far their blazing bunches to the sun,
A brown One, a hoofed One, pipes against the gale.
Up scrambled I then, furry fingers helping me.

I was on the mountain, wandering, wandering;
No one but the pine trees and the white birch knew.
Over rocks I scrambled, looked up and saw that Strange Thing,
Peaked ears and sharp horns, pricked against the blue.

Oh, and, how he piped there! piped upon the high reeds
Till the blue air crackled like a frost-film on a pool!
Oh, and how he spread himself, like a child whom no one heeds,
Tumbled chuckling in the brook, all sleek and kind and cool!

He had berries 'twixt his horns, crimson-red as cochineal.,
Bobbing, wagging wantonly they tickled him, and oh,
How his deft lips puckered round the reed, seemed to chase and steal
Sky-music, earth-music, tree-music low!

I said "Good-day, Thou!" He said, "Good-day, Thou!"
Wiped his reed against the spotted doe-skin on his back,
He said, "Come up here, and I will teach thee piping now.
While the earth is singing so, for tunes we shall not lack."

Up scrambled I then, furry fingers helping me.
Up scrambled I. So we sat beside the cairn.
Broad into my face laughed that horned Thing so naughtily.
Oh, it was a rascal of a woodland Satyr's bairn!

'So blow, and so, Thou! Move thy fingers faster, look!
Move them like the little leaves and whirling midges. So!
Soon `twill twist like tendrils and out-twinkle like the lost brook.
Move thy fingers merrily, and blow! Blow! Blow!"

Brown One! Hoofed One! Beat time to keep me straight.
Kick it on the red stone, whistle in my ear.
Brush thy crimson berries in my face, then hold thy breath, for - wait!
Joy comes bubbling to me lips. I pipe, oh, hear!

Blue sky, art glad of us? Green wood, art glad of us?
Old hard-heart mountain, dost thou hear me, how I blow?
Far away the sea-isles swim in sun-haze luminous.
Each one has a color like the seven-splendor bow.

Wind, wind, wind, dost thou mind me how I pipe, Now?
Chipmunk chatt'ring in the beech, rabbit in the brake?
Furry arm around my neck: "Oh, Thou art a brave one, Thou!"
Satyr, little satyr-friend, my heart with joy doth ache!

Sky-music, earth-music, tree-music tremulous,
Water over steaming rocks, water in the shade,
Storm-tune and sun-tune, how they flock up unto us,
Sitting by the red cairn, gay and unafraid!

Brown One, Hoofed One, give me nimble hoofs, Thou!
Give me furry fingers and a secret furry tail!

Pleasant are thy smooth horns: if their like were on my brow
Might I not abide here, till the strong sun fail?

Oh, the sorry brown eyes! Oh, the soft kind hand-touch,
Sudden brush of velvet ears across my wind-cool cheek!
"Play-mate, Pipe-mate, thou askest one good boon too much.
I could never find thee horns, though day-long I seek.

"Yet, keep the pipe, Thou: I will cut another one.
Keep the pipe and play on it for all the world to hear.
Ah, but it was good once to sit together in the sun!
Though I have but half a soul, it finds thee very dear!

"Wise Thing, Mortal Thing, yet my half-soul fears thee!
Take the pipe and go thy ways, quick now, for the sun
Reels across the hot west and stumbles dazzled to the sea.
Take the pipe, and oh-one kiss! then run, run, run! run!"

Silence on the mountain. Lonely stands the high cairn,
All the leaves a-shivering, all the stones dead-gray.
O thou cold small pipe, which way is fled that Satyr's bairn?
I am lost and all alone, and down drops the day.

I was on the mountain, wandering, wandering
There I got this Pipe o' dreams. Strange, when I blow,
Something deep as human love starts a-crying, troubling.
Is it only sky-music, earth-music low?

THE MIRAGE by NATHAN HASKELL DOLE
Across the Bay are low-lying cliffs,
Where stand fishermen's cottages:
I can barely distinguish them with the naked eye.
But to-day the cliffs are lifted, escarpt,
Perpendicular, mysterious, inaccessible,
And those sordid dwellings have become
The magnificent fortified castles of Sea-kings.

THE ROAD BEYOND THE TOWN by MICHAEL EARLS, S.J.
A road goes up a pleasant hill,
And a little house looks down:
Ah! but I see the roadway still
And the day I left the town.

The day I left my father's home,
It's many a year ago,
And a heart and hope were brave to roam
the long, long road I know.

The long, long road by hill and plain,
It's tired the heart might be:

But hope stayed bright in sun or rain,
And a Voice that called to me.

A Voice that called me over the hill
And out of the little town:
Ah! but I see the roadway still.
And the good house looking down.

The house that spake me never a No!
As I started brave away,
But said with a blessing, Go!
And followed me every day.

It followed me down the road of years,
For a father's heart is true,
And joy is sweet in a mother's tears
For the deeds her child may do.

The poor little deeds, all powerless
For the Kingdom of God would be,

Save in His mercy will He bless
The road that goes with me:

The road that left a pleasant hill,
Where a little house looks down:
Ah! but I bless the roadway still,
And the land beyond the town.

THE LILAC by WALTER PRICHARD EATON
The scent of lilac in the air
Hath made him drag his steps and pause
Whence comes this scent within the Square,
Where endless dusty traffic roars?
A push-cart stands beside the curb,
With fragrant blossoms laden high;
Speak low, nor stare, lest we disturb
His sudden reverie!

He sees us not, nor heeds the din
Of clanging car and scuffling throng;
His eyes see fairer sights within,
And memory hears the robin's song
As once it trilled against the day,
And shook his slumber in a room
Where drifted with the breath of May
The lilac's sweet perfume.

The heart of boyhood in him stirs;
The wonder of the morning skies,
Of sunset gold behind the firs,
Is kindled in his dreaming eyes:
How far off is this sordid place,
As turning from our sight away
He crushes to his hungry face
A purple lilac spray.

GOD, THROUGH HIS OFFSPRING NATURE, GAVE ME LOVE by CHARLES GIBSON

God, through his offspring Nature, gave me love,
Though man in opposition saith me nay,
And taketh from my heart its life to-day,
As through the valley of the world I rove.
Still unaccompanied, within the grove
That doth enamored beings hold at play,
My spirit must pursue its lonely way,
And strive to pluck some flowers that bloom above.
Oh, wherefore then doth Nature give desire
To have that which mankind may not possess,
And force him to endure on earth hell's fire,
And live in one perpetual distress?
Some evil power must such love inspire,
And with it masquerade in Cupid's dress!

TO MUSIC by MAUDE GORDON-ROBY

"Music, the language, the atmosphere of the Soul."

FLY back where Melodies like lilies grow,
My weary heart is bending low;

Fly higher yet to joyful realms above,
Where holy Angels dwell in love.

Fly higher still and hear the Angel throng
And bring to me their Glory-song:

Ah Music, thou and I above the World
May dwell where heaven with shining song is pearled!

While Sun and Moon and all the planets roll
I'll love thee, Music, language of my soul!

Music-lark from on high, song that doth fly,
Spark of the sky!

THE VOICE IN THE SONG by MARY GERTRUDE HAMILTON

High in the apple bough jauntily swinging,
Hid by the branches in bridal array,
Straight from his heart, all his life in his singing,
Chants a wee bird, lures his mate with his lay.
"Sweet, sweet, my sweet,
Hear I entreat!
Say, love, together, this bright sunny weather,
Gold of the west we shall weave in a nest!
Have no fear! Trust me, dear!
Sunshine of May that will gild every day
Pledge I to thee if thou'lt harken to me."

Lo! in the light thro' the gay branches streaming,
Quivering in answer to all the bird sings,
Warm on a breath, leaps a soul with love gleaming,
Speeds to its mate on its glittering wings.
"Dear, on thy breast
Earth yields its best!
Loud in the singing I heard thy call ringing,
Pleading and strong in the voice of the song,
Whisper low, Yes, just so!
Softly revealing the depth of thy feeling,
Words in whose fire glow thy love and desire."

HYMNS AND ANTHEMS SUNG AT WELLESLEY COLLEGE by CAROLINE HAZARD
I
MOUNT CARMEL
Where art Thou, O my Lord?
Mount Carmel saw the throng
Of priests and heard the song;
To Baal was their call
From morn till night did fall.

Where art Thou, O my Lord?
Again Mount Carmel heard
Not in the spoken word,
Not in the earthquake's shock,
Not in the thunder roll,
But in the inmost soul.

II
VESPER HYMN
Send peaceful sleep, O Lord, this night,
To keep us till the morning light;
And let no vision of alarm
Come near to do Thy children harm

Within Thy circling arms we lie,
O God, in Thine infinity;

Our souls in quiet shall abide
Beset with love on every side.

III
THIS IS THAT BREAD
This is that Bread that came down from Heaven,
he that eateth of this Bread shall live forever.

Bread on which angels feed,
Bread for the spirit's need
By faith receiving,
New life do Thou impart,
New strength to every heart,
Pure love of God Thou art
To us believing.

IV
O SLOW OF HEART
O slow of heart to believe! Ought Christ not to
have suffered these things and to enter into His Glory?

Quicken, Lord, my fainting heart,
Touch my eyes that they may see,
Let me know Thee as Thou art.
Life and Immortality.

V
ALL HAIL TO THEE, CHILD JESUS
All hail to Thee, child Jesus!
As the brooding darkness flies
At the swift approach of day,
Sun of righteousness, arise,
Chase the gloom of night away.
Great Prince of Peace, come to thine own,
And build in every heart Thy throne.

Come to shed Thy healing balm
On all nations of the earth,
Child Jesus, come with holy calm,
How we hail thy wondrous birth.
Great Prince of Peace, come to Thine own,
And build in every heart Thy throne.
All hail to Thee, Child Jesus!

VI
THE WINE-PRESS
Who is this that comes from Edom
In such glorious array,
With his festal garments gleaming,
Travelling on his royal way
With a face majestic, calm and grave?
I that speak in righteousness, mighty to save.

Why is thy apparel crimson,
Why is all thy garments' pride
Stained as in the time of vintage
And with blood-red-color dyed?
Because of helpers I had none
I have trodden the wine-press alone.

VII
WAKEN, SHEPHERDS!
(Angels) Hosanna! Hosanna! Hosanna!
(Shepherds) Waken, Shepherds, waken;
Whence this glowing light?
Ere the dawn of morning,
Solemn signs of warning
Portent of affright!

(Angels) Courage, Shepherds, courage!
Banish your dismay,
or ye all are saved.
In the town of David

Christ is born to-day.

(Shepherds) Harken, Shepherds, harken,
Hear the angels sing!
Jehovah sends a token,
He himself hath spoken
To proclaim our King.

(Angels) Hasten, Shepherds, hasten,
This shall be your sign;
Where the kine are stabled,
In a manger cradled
Lies the Child Divine.

(Shepherds and Angels) Angels, Shepherds, People,
Shout the glad refrain!
Joy to every nation
Bringing full salvation,
Christ has come to reign.
Hosanna! Hosanna! Hosanna!

REUBEN ROY by HAROLD CRAWFORD STEARNS

Little fellow, brown with wind
I saw him in the street
Peering at numbers on the posts,
But most discreet:

For when a woman came outdoors,
Or slyly peeped instead,
He turned away, took off his hat,
And scratched his head.

I watched him from my garden-wall
Perhaps an hour or more,
For something in his attitude,
The clothes he wore,

Awoke the dimmest memories
Of when I was a boy
And knew the story of a man
Named Reuben Roy.

It seems that Reuben went to sea
The night his wife decried
The fence he built before their house
And up the side.

He wanted it but she did not,
Because it hid from view
The spot in which her mignonette
And tulips grew.

Nobody saw his face again,
But each year, unawares,
He sent a sum for taxes due

And fence repairs.

My curiosity aroused,

I sauntered forth to see
Whether this individual
Were really he.

"Who are you looking for?" I asked
His eyes, like two bright pence,
Sparkled at mine; and then he said:
"A fence."

"Somebody burned it Hallowe'en,
When people were in bed;
Before the judge could prosecute,
The culprit fled."

Well, Reuben only touched his hat
And mumbled, "Thank you, Sir,"
And asked me whereabouts to find
A carpenter.

COUNTRY ROAD by MARIE LOUISE HERSEY
I can't forget a gaunt grey barn
Like a face without an eye
That kept recurring by field and tarn
Under a Cape Cod sky.

I can't forget a woman's hand,
Roughened and scarred by toil
That beckoned clear-eyed children tanned
By sun and wind and soil.

Beauty and hardship, bent and bound
Under the selfsame yoke:
Babies with bare knees plump and round
And stooping women folk.

WREATHS by CAROLYN HILLMAN
Red wreaths
Hang in my neighbor's window,
Green wreaths in my own.
On this day I lost my husband.
On this day you lost your boy.
On this day
Christ was born.
Red wreaths,
Green wreaths
Hang in Our Windows
Red for a bleeding heart,
Green for grave grass.
Mary, mother of Jesus,

Look down and comfort us.
You too knew passion;
You too knew pain.
Comfort us,
Who are not brides of God,
Nor bore God.
On Christmas day
Hang wreaths,
Red for new pain.
Green for spent passion.

MEMPHIS by GORDON MALHERBE HILLMAN

WHY should I sing of my present? It is nothing to me or you,

Rather I'd dream of Dixie and tie ships on the old bayou!
Rather I'd dream of my packets and the lazy river days,
Rather I'd dream of my levee and the crimson sunset haze,

Rather I'd dream of my triumphs, of the days that are long gone by,
Rather I'd dream of flame-tipped stacks against a saffron sky,
Of level lawns of topaz, of level fields of jade,
Of the rambling pillared mansions that my fathers' fathers made!

Why should I sing of my present? It is nothing to you or me,
But the river road, the great road, the high road to the sea!
Aye, that is worth the dreaming, aye, that was worth the pain.
Send me back my river, and I shall wake again!

SAINT COLUMBKILLE by E. J. V. HUIGINN

Columbkille! Saint Columbkille!
You naughty man, Saint Columbkille!
Why did you Finnian's Psalter take
And secretly a copy make?
You know 'twas such a naughty thing
For one descended from a king
To lock himself into a cell,
'Twas far from right,-you knew it well,
And copy Finnian's Psalter through,
Against his will as well you knew.
And then to think a common bird
Should feel such shame, that when he heard
The breathing spy outside your door,
And felt your sainthood was no more,
Should through the crack attack the spy,
And in a rage pluck out his eye,
As if that saintly Irish crane
Would hide from all your Saintship's stain.
I grieve to think that you did add
Sin unto sin; it is too bad.
For Finnian could not you persuade
To yield the copy that you made,
Until the King in his behalf
Ruled-"To each cow belongs her calf":

And then you grew so mad you swore
On Erin's face you'd look no more.
And crossed the sea the Picts to save,
Because you so did misbehave
To dear Saint Finnian: faith, 'twas ill
For you to act so, Columbkille!
A saint you were no doubt, no doubt!
What pity 'twas you were found out!
We know an angel (snob or fool?)

To Kiaran showed a common rule,
An axe, an auger, and a saw,
And told that saint it was the law
Of Heaven that Columbkille should be
Far, far above such saints as he;
For Columbkille contemned a crown,
While he these homely tools laid down,
To serve the Lord, and that the Lord
To each would give his due reward.
I wonder if that angel knew
That Christ these tools had laid down too.
O Columbkille! O Columbkille!
A saint like you must have his will,
But for myself I'd rather be
The common sinner that you see
Than make a crane ashamed of me,
And angels talk such idiocy.

MISS DOANE by WINIFRED VIRGINIA JACKSON
Miss Doane was sixty, probably;
She rented third floor room
That opened on an airshaft full
Of cooking smells and gloom.

She worked in philanthropic man's
Well-known department store;
Cashiered in basement, hot and close,
For forty years or more.

Each night when she came home she'd stand
A moment in the hall,
Before she went into her room
With low and tender call.

And often I would hear her voice
Repeat a childish prayer;
Or read some old, old fairy tale
Of Princess, grand and fair.

One night I went to visit her
And spied, in little chair
A great wax doll, in dainty dress,
And curls of flaxen hair.

I praised the doll; its prettiness;

Miss Doane said, "I'm alone.
She comforts me. I wanted so
A child to call my own."

Each night I heard her softly sing
A childish lullaby;
But once, and just before she died,
I heard her cry and cry!

FALLEN FENCES by WINIFRED VIRGINIA JACKSON
THE woods grew dark; black shadows
rocked
And I could scarcely see
My way along the old tote road,
That long had seemed to me

To wind on aimlessly; but now
Came full to life; the rain
Would soon strike down; ahead I saw
A clearing, and a lane

Between gray, fallen fences and
Wide, grayer, grim stone walls;
So grim and gray I shrank from thought
Of weary, aching spalles.

On stony knoll great aspens swayed
And swung in browsing teeth
Of wind; slim, silvered yearlings shook
And shivered underneath.

Beyond, some ancient oak trees bent
And wrangled over roof
Of weatherbeaten house, and barn
Whose sag bespoke no hoof.

And ivy crawled up either end
Of house, to chimney, where
It lashed in futile anger at
The wind wolves of the air.

I thought the house abandoned, and
I ran to get inside,
When suddenly the old front door
was opened and flung wide

And she stood there, with hand on knob,
As I went swiftly in,
Then closed the door most softly on
The storm and shrieking din.

A space I stood and looked at her,
So young; 'twas passing strange
That fifty years or more had gone

And brought no new style's change.

The sweetness, daintiness of her
In starched and dotted gown
Of creamy whiteness, over hoops,
With ruffles winding down!

We had not much to say, and yet
Of words I felt no lack;
Her smiles slipped into dimples, stopped
A moment, then dropped back.

I felt her pride of race; her taste
In silken rug and chair,
And quaintly fashioned furniture
Of patterns old and rare.

On window sill a rose bush stood;
'Twas bringing rose to bud;
One full bloomed there but yesterday,
Dropped petals, red as blood.

Quite soon, she asked to be excused
For just a moment, and
Went out, returning with a tray
In either slender hand.

My glance could not but linger on
Each thin and lovely cup;
"This came, dear thing, from home!" she sighed
The while she raised it up.

And when the storm was done and I
Arose, reluctantly
To go, she too was loath to have
Me go, it seemed to me.

When I reached old Joe Webber's place,
Upon the Corner Road,
I went into the Upper Field
Where Joe, round-shouldered, hoed

Potatoes, culling them with hoe
And practised, calloused hand,
In rounded piles that brownly glowed
Upon the fresh-turned land.

"Say, Joe," I said, "who is that girl
With beauty's smiling charm,
That lives beyond that hemlock growth,
On that old grown-up farm?"

Joe listened, while I told him where
I'd been that afternoon,
Then straightened from his hoe, and hummed,
Before he spoke, a tune

"They cum ter thet old place ter live
Some sixty years ago;
Jest where they cum from, who they ware,
Wy, no one got to know.

"An' then, one day, he hired Hen's
Red racker an' the gig;
We never heard from him nor could
We track the hoss or rig.

"Hen waited 'bout a week, an' then
He went ter see the Wife;
He found her in thet settin' room:
She'd taken of her life.

"An' no one's lived in thet house sence;
Some say 'tis haunted,-but
I ain't no use fer foolishness,
So all I say's tut! tut!"

CROSS-CURRENTS by WINIFRED VIRGINIA JACKSON
They wrapped my soul in eiderdown;
They placed me warm and snug
In carved chair; set me with care
Upon an old prayer rug.

They cased my feet in golden shoes
That hurt at toe and heel;
My restless feet, with youth all fleet,
Nor asked how they might feel.

And now they wonder where I am,
And search with shrill, cold cry;
But I crouch low where tall reeds grow,
And smile as they pass by!

THE FAREWELL by WINIFRED VIRGINIA JACKSON
What is more beautiful
Than thought, soul-fed,
That I may be the crimson of a rose
When dead?

My soul, so light a joy
And grief will be,
That it will gently press the brown earth down
On me.

SONG by OLIVER JENKINS
Let me be great, as stars are great,
Singing of love, not of hate.

Love for sweet and simple things,
Like clouds and sea-shell whisperings,

Cool autumn winds, pale dew-kissed flowers,
Thin coils of smoke and granite towers,

Snow-capped mountain peaks that flash
High above a river's crash,

Shrill songs of birds and children's laughter,
Soft grey shadows trailing after

Sunbeam sprites that seek the woods
And lose themselves in solitudes.

All these I'll love, never hate,
And loving them, I will be great.

LOVE AUTUMNAL by OLIVER JENKINS
MY love will come in autumn-time
When leaves go spinning to the ground
And wistful stars in heaven chime
With the leaves' sound.

Then, we shall walk through dusty lanes
And pause beneath low-hanging boughs,
And there, while soft-hued beauty reigns
We'll make our vows.

Let others seek in spring for sighs
When love flames forth from every seed;
But love that blooms when nature dies
Is love indeed!

ECHOS by RUTH LAMBERT JONES
Traveling at dusk the noisy city street,
I listened to the newsboys' strident cries
Of "Extra," as with flying feet,
They strove to gain this man or that-their prize.
But one there was with neither shout nor stride,
And, having bought from him, I stood nearby,
Pondering the cruel crutches at his side,
Blaming the crowd's neglect, and wondering why

When suddenly I heard a gruff voice greet
The cripple with "On time to-night?"
Then, as he handed out the sheet,
The Youngster's answer-"You're all right.
My other reg'lars are a little late.
They'll find I'm short one paper when they come;
You see, a strange guy bought one in the wait,
I tho't 'twould cheer him up-he looked so glum!"

So, sheepishly I laughed, and went my way
For I had found a city's heart that day.

"German Retreat From Arras"
"Official Films"-they came
After "Corinne and Her Minstrels"
Had ministered to fame.

After "Corinne and Her Minstrels"
Had pigeon-toed away,
We saw where bits of churches
And bits of horses lay.

We saw bleak desolation;
We saw no unscathed tree.
We shivered in our comfort
And murmured: "Can it be!"

But later, walking homeward,
Repeating: "Is it true?"
We brushed a khaki shoulder
And asked no more. We knew!

When I was but a young lad,
And that is long ago,
I thought that luck loved every man,
And time his only foe,
And love was like a hawthorn bush
That blossomed every May,
And had but to choose his flower,
For that's the young lad's way.

Oh, youth's a thriftless squanderer,
It's easy come and spent,
And heavy is the going now
Where once the light foot went.
The hawthorn bush puts on its white,
The throstle whistles clear,
But Spring comes once for every man
Just once in all the year.

Such quiet sleep has come to them!
The Springs and Autumns pass,
Nor do they know if it be snow
Or daisies in the grass.

All day the birches bend to hear

The river's undertone;
Across the hush a fluting thrush
Sings even-song alone.

But down their dream there drifts no sound,
The winds may sob and stir:
On the still breast of Peace they rest
And they are glad of her.

They ask not any gift, they mind
Nor any foot that fares,
Unheededly life passes by
Such quiet sleep is theirs.

OLD LIZETTE ON SLEEP by AGNES LEE

Bed is the boon for me!
It's well to bake and sweep,
But hear the word of old Lizette:
It's better than all to sleep.

Summer and flowers are gay,
And morning light and dew;
But aged eyelids love the dark
Where never a light peeps through.

What! open-eyed, my dears?
Thinking your hearts will break.
There's nothing, nothing, nothing, I say,
That's worth the lying awake!

I learned it in my youth
Love I was dreaming of!
I learned it from the needle-work
That took the place of love.
I learned it from the years
And what they brought about;
From song, and from the hills of joy
Where sorrow sought me out.

It's good to dream and turn,
And turn and dream, or fall
To comfort with my pack of bones,
And know of nothing at all!

Yes, never know at all!
If prowlers mew or bark,
Nor wonder if it's three o'clock
Or four o'clock of the dark.

When the longer shades have fallen
And the last weariness
Has brought the sweetest gift of life,
The last forgetfulness.

If a sound as of old leaves

Stir the last bed I keep,
Then say, my dears: "It's old Lizette
She's turning in her sleep!"

MOTHERHOOD by AGNES LEE

Mary, the Christ long slain, passed silently.
Following the children joyously astir
Under the cedrus and the olive tree,
Pausing to let their laughter float to her.
Each voice an echo of a voice more dear,
She saw a little Christ in every face;
When lo, another woman, gliding near,
Yearned o'er the tender life that filled the place.
And Mary sought the woman's hand, and spoke:
"I know thee not, yet know thy memory tossed
With all a thousand dreams their eyes evoke
Who bring to thee a child beloved and lost.

"I, too, have rocked my little one,
O, He was fair!
Yea, fairer than the fairest sun,
And like its rays through amber spun
His sun-bright hair.
Still I can see it shine and shine."
"Even so," the woman said, "was mine."

"His ways were ever darling ways,"
And Mary smiled,
"So soft, so clinging! Glad relays
Of love were all His precious days.
My little child!
My infinite star! My music fled!"
"Even so was mine," the woman said.

Then whispered Mary: "Tell me, thou,
Of thine." And she:
"O, mine was rosy as a boug

Blooming with roses, sent, somehow,
To bloom for me!
His balmy fingers left a thrill
Within my breast that warms me still."

Then gazed she down some wilder, darker hour,
And said, when Mary questioned, knowing not,
"Who art thou, mother of so sweet a flower?"
"I am the mother of Iscariot."

ESSEX by GEORGE CABOT LODGE
I
Thy hills are kneeling in the tardy spring,
And wait, in supplication's gentleness,

The certain resurrection that shall bring
A robe of verdure for their nakedness.
Thy perfumed valleys where the twilights dwell,
Thy fields within the sunlight's living coil

Now promise, while the veins of nature swell,
Eternal recompense to human toil.
And when the sunset's final shades depart
The aspiration to completed birth
Is sweet and silent; as the soft tears start,
We know how wanton and how little worth
Are all the passions of our bleeding heart
That vex the awful patience of the earth.

II
Thine are the large winds and the splendid sun
Glutting the spread of heaven to the floor
Of waters rhythmic from far shore to shore,
And thine the stars, revealing one by one,
Thine the grave, lucent night's oblivion,
The tawny moon that waits below the skies,
Strange as the dawn that smote their blistered eyes
Who watched from Calvary when the Deed was done.
And thine the good brown earth that bares its breast
To thy benign October, thine the trees
Lusty with fruitage in the late year's rest;

And thine the men whos@ blood has glorified
Thy name with Liberty Is divine decrees
The men who loved thy soil and fought and died.

III
Toward thine Eastern window when the morn
Steals through the silver mesh of silent stars,
I come unlaurelled from the strenuous wars
Where men have fought and wept and died
Forlorn.

But here, across the early fields of corn,
The living silence dwelleth, and the gray
Sweet earth-mist, while afar the lisp of spray
Breathes from the ocean like a Triton's horn.
Open thy lattice, for the gage is won
For which this earth has journeyed though the dust
Of shattered systems, cold about the sun;
And proved by sin, by mighty lives impearled,
A voice cries through the sunrise: "Time is Just!"
And falls like dew God's pity on the world

THE SONG OF THE WAVE by GEORGE CABOT LODGE
This is the song of the wave! The mighty one!
Child of the soul of silence, beating the air to sound:
White as a live terror, as a drawn sword,
This is the wave.

II
This is the song of the wave, the white-maned steed of the Tempest
Whose veins are swollen with life,
In whose flanks abide the four winds.
This is the wave.

III
This is the song of the wave! The dawn leaped out of the sea
And the waters lay smooth as a silver shield,
And the sun-rays smote on the waters like a golden sword.
Then a wind blew out of the morning
And the waters rustled
And the wave was born!

IV
This is the song of the wave! The wind blew out of the noon
And the white sea-birds like driven foam
Winged in from the ocean that lay beyond the sky
And the face of the waters was barred with white,
For the wave had many brothers,
And the wave was strong!

V
This is the song of the wave! The wind blew out of the sunset
And the west was lurid as Hell.
The black clouds closed like a tomb, for the sun was dead.
Then the wind smote full as the breath of God,
And the wave called to its brothers,
"This is the crest of life!"

VI
This is the song of the wave, that rises to fall,
Rises a sheer green wall like a barrier of glass
That has caught the soul of the moonlight.
Caught and prisoned the moon-beams;
Its edge is frittered to foam.
This is the wave!

VII
This is the song of the wave, of the wave that falls
Wild as a burst of day-gold blown through the colours of morning
It shivers to infinite atoms up the rumbling steep of sand.
This is the wave.

VIII
This is the song of the wave that died in the fullness of life.
The prodigal this, that lavished its largess of strength
In the lust of attainment.
Aiming at things for Heaven too high,
Sure in the pride of life, in the richness of strength.
So tried it the impossible height, till the end was found:
Where ends the soul that yearns for the fillet of morning stars,
The soul in the toils of the journeying worlds,
Whose eye is filled with the Image of God,
And the end is Death!

Dearest, we are like two flowers
Blooming in the garden,
A purple aster flower and a red one
Standing alone in a withered desolation.

The garden plants are shattered and seeded,
One brittle leaf scrapes against another,
Fiddling echoes of a rush of petals.
Now only you and I nodding together.

Many were with us; they have all faded.
Only we are purple and crimson,
Only we in the dew-clear mornings,
Smarten into color as the sun rises.

When I scarcely see you in the flat moonlight,
And later when my cold roots tighten,
I am anxious for morning,
I cannot rest in fear of what may happen.

You or I-and I am a coward.
Surely frost should take the crimson.
Purple is a finer color,

Very splendid in isolation.

So we nod above the broken
Stems of flowers almost rotted.
Many mornings there cannot be now
For us both. Ah, Dear, I love you!

PATTERNS by AMY LOWELL
I walk down the garden paths,
And all the daffodils
Are blowing, and the bright blue squills.
I walk down the patterned garden paths
In my stiff, brocaded gown.
With my powdered hair and jewelled fan,
I too am a rare
Pattern. As I wander down
The garden paths.

My dress is richly figured,
And the train
Makes a pink and silver stain
On the gravel, and the thrift
Of the borders.
Just a plate of current fashion,
Tripping by in high-heeled, ribboned shoes.
Not a softness anywhere about me,
Only a whale-bone and brocade.

And I sink on a seat in the shade
Of a lime tree. For my passion
Wars against the stiff brocade.
The daffodils and squills
Flutter in the breeze
As they please.
And I weep;
For the lime tree is in blossom
And one small flower has dropped upon my bosom.

And the splashing of waterdrops
In the marble fountain
Comes down the garden paths.
The dripping never stops.
Underneath my stiffened gown
Is the softness of a woman bathing in a marble basin,
A basin in the midst of hedges grown
So thick, she cannot see her lover hiding,
But she guesses he is near,
And the sliding of the water
Seems the stroking of a dear
Hand upon her.
What is Summer in a fine brocaded gown!
I should like to see it lying in a heap upon the ground.
All the pink and silver crumpled up upon the ground.

I would be the pink and silver as I ran along the paths,
And he would stumble after,
Bewildered by my laughter.
I should see the sun flashing from his sword hilt and the buckles
on his shoes.
I would choose
To lead him in a maze along the patterned paths,
A bright and laughing maze for my heavy-booted lover,
Till he caught me in the shade,
And the buttons of his waistcoat bruised my body as he clasped me,
Aching, melting, unafraid.
With the shadows of the leaves and the sundrops,
And the plopping of the waterdrops,
All about us in the open afternoon
I am very like to swoon
With the weight of this brocade,
For the sun sifts through the shade.

Underneath the fallen blossom
In my bosom,
Is a letter I have hid.
It was brought to me this morning by a rider from
the Duke.
"Madam, we regret to inform you that Lord Hartwell
Died in action Thursday sen'night."
As I read it in the white morning sunlight.
The letters squirmed like snakes.
"Any answer, Madam," said my footman.
"No," I told him.
"See that the messenger takes some refreshment.
No, no answer."

And I walked into the garden,
Up and down the patterned paths,
In my stiff, correct brocade.
The blue and yellow flowers stood up proudly in
the sun,
Each one.
I stood upright too,
Held rigid to the pattern
By the stiffness of my gown.
Up and down I walked,
Up and down.

In a month he would have been my husband,
In a month, here, underneath this lime,
We would have broke the pattern;
He for me, and I for him,
He as Colonel, I as lady,
On this shady seat.
He had a whim
That sunlight carried blessing.
And I answered, "It shall be as you have said."

Now he is dead.

In Summer and in Winter I shall walk
Up and down
The patterned garden paths
In my stiff, brocaded gown.
The squills and the daffodils
Will give place to pillared roses, and to asters, and to snow.

I shall go
Up and down,
In my gown.
Gorgeously arrayed,
Boned and stayed.
And the softness of my body will be guarded from
embrace
By each button, hook and lace.
For the man who should loose me is dead,
Fighting with the Duke in Flanders,
In a pattern called a war.
Christ! What are patterns for?

A BATHER by AMY LOWELL
Thick dappled by circles of sunshine and fluttering shade.
Your bright, naked body advances, blown over by leaves,
Half-quenched in their various green, just a point
Of you showing,
A knee or a thigh, sudden glimpsed, then at once
Blotted into
The filmy and flickering forest, to start out again
Triumphant in smooth, supple roundness, edged
Sharp as white ivory,
Cool, perfect, with rose rarely tinting your lips and

Your breasts,
Swelling out from the green in the opulent curves
Of ripe fruit,
And hidden, like fruit, by the swift intermittence
Of leaves.
So, clinging to branches and moss, you advance on the ledges
Of rock which hang over the stream, with the wood-smells about you,
The pungence of strawberry plants and of gum-oozing spruces,
While below runs the water impatient, impatient to take you,
To splash you, to run down your sides, to sing you of deepness,
Of pools brown and golden, with brown-and-gold flags on their borders,
Of blue, lingering skies floating solemnly over your beauty,
Of undulant waters a-sway in the effort to hold you

To keep you submerged and quiescent while over you glories
The summer.
Oread, Dryad, or Naiad, or just
Woman, clad only in youth and in gallant perfection,
Standing up in a great burst of sunshine, you dazzle my eyes
Like a snow-star, a moon, your effulgence burns up in a halo,
For you are the chalice which holds all the races of men.
You slip into the pool and the water folds over your shoulder,
And over the tree-tops the clouds slowly follow
your swimming, To behold the way they act.
And the scent of the woods is sweet on this hot
summer morning.

LEPRECHAUNS AND CLURICAUNS by DENIS A. MCCARTHY
Over where the Irish hedges
Are with blossoms white as snow,
Over where the limestone ledges
Through the soft green grasses show
There the fairies may be seen
In their jackets of red and green,
Leprechauns and cluricauns,
And the other ones, I ween.

And, bedad, it is a wonder
To behold the way they act.
They're the lads that seldom blunder,
Wise and wary, that's the fact.
You may hold them with your eye;
Look away and off they fly;
Leprechauns and cluricauns,
Bedad, but they are sly!

They have heaps of golden treasure
Hid away within the ground,
Where they spend their days in leisure,
And where fairy joys abound;
But to mortals not a guinea
Will they give-no, not a penny.
Leprechauns and cluricauns,
Their gold is seldom found.

Maybe of a morning early
As you pass a lonely rath,
You may see a little curly
Headed fairy in your path.
He'll be working at a shoe,

But he'll have his eye on you
Leprechauns and cluricauns,
They know just what to do.

Visions of a life of riches
Surely will before you flash;
(You'll no longer dig the ditches,
You'll be well supplied with cash.)
And you'll seize the little man,
And you'll hold him, if you can;
Leprechauns and cluricauns,
'Tis they're the slipp'ry clan!

L'ENVOI by DOROTHEA LAWRENCE MANN
When the time for parting comes, and the day is on the wane,
And the silent evening darkens over hill and over plain,
And earth holds no more sorrow, no more grief, and no more pain,
Shall we weary for the battle and the strife?

When at last the trail is ending, and the stars are growing near,
And we breathe the breath of conquest, and the voices that we hear
Are the great companions' voices that have hallowed year on year,
Shall we know an instant's grieving as we pass?

Shall we pause a fleeting moment ere we grasp the eager hands,
Take one last long look of wonder at the dimming of the lands,
Love the earth one glowing moment ere we pass from its demands,
Cull all beauty in its essence as we gaze?

Or with not one backward longing shall we leap the last abyss,
Scale the highest crags glad-hearted, fearful only lest the bliss
Of an earth-remembering instant should delay the great sun's kiss
Consuming us within the flame?

TO IMAGINATION, SUGGESTED BY MAXFIELD PARRISH'S "AIR CASTLES" by
DOROTHEA LAWRENCE MANN
O Beauteous boy a-dream, what visions
sought
Of pictures magical thy eyes unfold,
What triumphs of celestial wonders wrought,
What marvels from a breath of beauty rolled!
Skyward and seaward on the clouds are scrolled,
A mystic imagery of castled thought,
A thousand worlds to lose, or win and mould
A radiant iridescence swiftly caught
Of ever-changing glory, fancy-fraught.

Blue wonder of the sea and luminous sky,
A thousand wonders in thy dreamlit face,
Eyes that behold afar the turrets high
Of Ilium, and the transient mortal grace
Of Deirdre's sadness, all the conquering race
Of Athens, eyes that saw Eden's beauty lie
In passionate adoration visions trace
Across the tender brooding of the sigh
That wrecked a city and made chieftains die.

Forward not backward turns the mystic shine
Of those far-seeing orbs that track the gleam
The fleecy marvel of the cloud is line
On line the wizard tracery of a dream.
O lad, who buildest not of things that seem,
Beyond what bounds of visioning divine
Came that far smile, from what long-strayed sun-beam
Caught thou the radiance, from what fostering vine
The power to build and mould the deep design?

Knowest thou the secret that thy brush would tell,
Is all the dream a bubbled splendor white,
Beyond those castles cloud-bound, does there dwell
The eternal silence of the dark or light?
Will thy hand hold the pen which shall indict
The symboled mystery-write the final knell
Of rainbow fancy-is the distant sight
A nothingless encircled by a spell
Of gleaming bubbles wrought of beauty's shell?

In vain to question, where the mystery
Of Youth's short golden dream is lord and king.
The eyes that farthest gaze in ecstasy,
Were never meant to paint the immortal thing
They see, nor understand the joy they bring.
The misty baubles of the sky and sea
Sail on. Dream still, bright-visioned boy, and fling
The glittering mantle of thy thoughts that flee,
Weaving us evermore thy shining pageantry.

DRAGON by JEANNETTE MARKS "THE BOOKMAN."
Somr saw a dragon eating up the light,
Oho! Oho! Oho, ho, ho!
Some heard a lost bird riding out the night,
Oho! Oho! Oho, ho, ho!

But I saw:
A low dark hill with its twisted back
Two wings of flame from the green cloud rack,
A sprawling flank overlaid with leaf
Glitter and gleam and shine like steel,
Crackle and lash like a serpent's tail!

And I heard:
The wind draw out of the west and wail,

Dance and stagger and jig and reel!
With the long low sound of a life in grief!

I saw a life in grief
Oho! Oho! Oho, ho, ho
Dance and stagger and jig and reel!
Oho! Oho! Oho, ho, ho!

GREEN GOLDEN DOOR by JEANNETTE MARKS "THE BOOKMAN."
Green golden door, swing in, swing in!
Fanning the life a man must live,
Echoes and airs and minstrelsies,
Love and hope that he called his,
Fear and hurt and a man's own sin
Casting them forth and sucking them in,
Green golden door, swing out, swing out!

Green golden door, swing in, swing in!
Show me the youth that will not die,
Tell me the dream that has not waked,
Seek me the heart that never ached,
Green golden door, swing out, swing out!

Green golden door, swing in, swing out!
Long is the wailing of man's breath,
Short is the wail of death.

SLEEPY HOLLOW, CONCORD by JOHN CLAIR MINOT
Four graves there are upon the wooded crest,
Each one a shrine to pilgrims ever dear.
Uncovered, mute, are those who tarry here.
Romance's dreaming master lies at rest
Beneath the cedars. Near is one whose breast
Held Mother Nature's lore. Beyond, the seer
And sage. There, one who saw her duty clear,
Her name by little men and women blessed.

Four friends who walked in Concord's pleasant ways
Long years ago. They dwelt and worked apart,
But now the world has crowned them with its bays,
And holds them close forever to its heart.
O, sacred hill! There Genius, guarding stays,
And from its slopes shall never Love depart!

THE SWORD OF ARTHUR by JOHN CLAIR MINOT
A castle stands in Yorkshire
(Oh, the hill is fair and green!)
And far beneath it lies a cave
No living man has seen.

It is the cave enchanted

(Oh, seek it ere ye die!)
And there King Arthur and his knights
In dreamless slumber lie.

One time a peasant found it
(Oh, the years have hurried well!)
It was the day of fate for him,
And this is what befell:

Upon a couch of crystal
(Oh, heart be pure and strong!)
He saw the King, and, close beside,
The armored knights athrong.

And all of them were sleeping
(Praise God, who sendeth rest!)
The sleep that comes when strife is done
And ended every quest.

Beside the good King Arthur
(How high is your desire?)
His sword within its scabbard lay,
The sword with blade of fire.

Now had the peasant known it
(Oh, if we all could know!)

He should have drawn that wondrous blade
Before he turned to go.

If but his hand had touched it
(The sword still lieth there!)
He would have felt in every vein
A lofty purpose thrill.
If but his hand had drawn it
(The sword still lieth there!)
A kingly way he would have walked,
Wherever he might fare.
But no; he fled affrighted
(Oh, pitiful the cost!)
And then he knew; but lo! the way
Into the cave was lost.

He searched forever after
(All this was long ago!)
But nevermore that crystal cave
His eager eyes could know.

Pray God ye have the vision
(Oh, search in every land!)
To seize the sword that Arthur bore
When it lies at your hand.

THE DIVINE FOREST by CHARLES R. MURPHY
If there be leaves on the forest floor,

Dead leaves there are and nothing more,
If trunks of trees seem sentinels,
For what their vigil no man tells.
And if you clasp these guardian trees
Nothing there is to hurt or please;
Only the dead roof of the forest drops
Gently down and never stops
And roofs you in and roofs you under,
Mute and away from life's dim thunder;
And if there come eternal spring
It is but more disheartening,
For Autumn takes the Spring and Summer
Autumn that is the latest comer
With the Springtime's misty wonder
And the Summer's yield of gold,
Weighs you down and weighs you under
To where the blackened leaves are mold. . .
The lone gift of the forest is ever new:
Eternity where dwell not you.
The forest, accepting, heeds you not;
Accepting all-you are forgot.
If there be leaves on the forest floor,
Dead leaves there are and nothing more.

Once the forest spoke but now is silent,
Save in the skyward branches whence no sound
Seems to touch ear of any man below
Or else no longer the man knows how to hear.
Such men build roofs to keep the forest out,
Yet all their roofs are built of the forest's self;

Only they make the dead tree a shield against the
living.
Such lapsing of the forest then they use
And turn it into countless lowly dwellings;
Sometimes they even cut the living down
To leaven the dead roofs they would erect.
Though some of these low roofs are lovely there
Beneath the guardianship of forest trees,
And some yearn upward as with thought of wings,
Yet the eyes of the dwellers therein are dark
To the upper forest and they
Fearful of the windy freedom of its top.
They have forgotten
That the greatest roof is but a banner
And that it was a tree that made a Cross.

MAGIC, TO W.S.B. by EDWARD J. O'BRIEN
I ran into the sunset light
As hard as I could run:
The treetops bowed in sheer delight
As if they loved the sun:
And all the songs of little birds
Who laughed and cried in silver words
Were joined as they were one.

And down the streaming golden sky
A lark came circling with a cry
Of wonder-weaving joy:
And all the arch of heaven rang
Where meadowlands of dreaming hang
As when I was a boy.

And through the ringing solitude
In pulsing lovely amplitude
A mist hung in a shroud,
As though the light of loneliness
Turned pure delight to holiness,
And bathed it in a cloud.

I stripped my laughing body bare
And plunged into that holy air
That washed me like a sea,
And raced against its silver tide
That stroked my eager glancing side
And made my spirit free.

Across the limits of the land
The wind and I swept hand and hand
Beyond the golden glow.
We danced across the ocean plain
Like thrushes singing in the rain
A song of long ago.

And on into the silver night
We strove to win the race with light
And bring the vision home,
And bring the wonder home again
Unto the sleeping eyes of men
Across the singing foam.

And down the river of the world
Our glowing, limbs in glory swirled
As spring within a flower,
And stars in music of delight
Streamed gayly down our shoulders white
Like petals in a shower.

And tears of awful wonder ran
Adown my cheeks to hear the clan
Of beauty chaunting white
The prayer too deep for living word,
Or sight of man or winging bird,
Or music over forest heard
At falling of the night.

And dropping slowly as the dew
On grasses that the winds renew
In urge of flooding fire,
And softly as the hushing boughs
The gentle airs of dawn arouse

To cradle morning's quire.

The murmur of the singing leaves
Around the secret Flame,
Like mating swallows 'neath the eaves
In rustling silence came,
And flowing through the silent air
Creation fluttered in a prayer
Descending on a spiral stair,
And calling me by name.

It nestled in my dreaming eyes
Like heaven in a lake,
And softened hope into surprise
For very beauty's sake,
And silence blossomed into morn,
Whose fragrant rosy-breasted dawn
Could scarcely bear to break.

I sang into the morning light
As loud as I could sing,
The treetops bowed in sheer delight
Before the slanting wing.
And all the songs of little birds
Who laughed and cried in silver words
Adored the Risen Spring.

MICHAEL PAT - TO ANNA HEMPSTEAD BRANCH by EDWARD J. O'BRIEN
Old Michael Pat he said to me
He saw an angel in a tree.
He knew I'd never, never doubt him,
For what would heaven be without them.
The angel laughed for very glee
And sang out loud: "Heigh! come with me!"
Old Michael felt a creeping kind
Of wonder in his humble mind,
And, hardly knowing what to say,
Ran where the angel showed the way.
The lambs were running on the hills,
Glad laughter echoed from the rills,
And many hidden little birds
Talked pleasant things in singing words.
He followed up a mountain then
And saw a crowd of singing men
Approaching to a Crown of Light
Wherein they took a fresh delight.
He danced and sang and whooped and crew
To see the Lord of all he knew
Surrounded by the living songs
Of stars and men in countless throngs,
And then he died to life again,
And shovelled with the strength of ten.
He taught me how to say my letters,
And take my hat off to my betters,
And when I asked for fairy stories,

He told me of angelic glories.
He was a lovely farmer, he
Had seen an angel in a tree.

SONG. FROM "FLESH: A GEOGORIAN ODE" by EDWARD J. O'BRIEN
Ebb on with me across the sunset tide
And float beyond the waters of the world,
The light of evening slipping from my side,
Thy softened voice in waves of silence furled.

Flow on into the flaming morning wine,
Drowning the land in color. Then on high
Rise in thy candid innocence and shine
Like to a poplar straight against the sky.

IN MEMORIAM: FRANCIS LEDWIDGE (Killed in action, July 31, 1917) by NORREYS JEPHSON O'CONOR
Soldier and singer of Erin,
What may I fashion for thee?
What garland of words or of flowers?
Singer of sunlight and showers,
The wind on the lea;

Of clouds, and the houses of Erin,
Wee cabins, white on the plain,
And bright with the colours of even,
Beauty of earth and of heaven falls
Outspread beyond Slane!
night through let my mind be still,

Slane, where the Easter of Patrick
Flamed on the night of the Gael,
Guard both the honor and story
Of him who has died for the glory
That crowns Innisfail.

Soldier of right and of freedom,
I offer thee song and hot tears.
With Brian, and Red Hugh O'Donnell,
The chiefs of Tyrone and Tryconnell,
Live on through the years!

EVENSONG by NORREYS JEPHSON O'CONOR
A shepherd piping, herald of the Night
Who comes with Silence up the coloured vale,
Treading low gently, clad in greyish white,
Poignantly piping, sound your reedy wail!
For Day departed moves in funeral train
Tended by Twilight and, in deepest rose,
The splendid Sunset melts beneath the main

While sweet the Sea-wind with cool softness blows.
As when a mother gathers to her breast
The child who frets for Dad's remembered smart,
Now Light fades quickly in the ashen west,
And Night-Peace falls across my troubled heart.
Flutes, for the night through let my mind be still,
And God keep safe with Him my stubborn will!

THE PROPHET by JOSEPHINE PRESTON PEABODY

All day long he kept the sheep:
Far and early, from the crowd,
On the hills from steep to steep,
Where the silence cried aloud;
And the shadow of the cloud
Wrapt him in a noonday sleep.

Where he dipped the water's cool,
Filling boyish hands from thence,
Something breathed across the pool
Stir of sweet enlightenments;
And he drank, with thirsty sense,
Till his heart was brimmed and full.

Still, the hovering Voice unshed,
And the Vision unbeheld,
And the mute sky overhead,
And his longing, still withheld!
Even when the two tears welled,
Salt, upon that lonely bread.

Vaguely blessed in the leaves,
Dim-companioned in the sun,
Eager mornings, wistful eyes,
Very hunger drew him on;
And To-morrow ever shone
With the glow the sunset weaves.

Even so, to that young heart,
Words and hands and Men were dear;
And the stir of lane and mart
After daylong vigil here.
Sunset called, and he drew near,
Still to find his path apart.

When the Bell, with gentle tongue,
Called the herd-bells home again,
Through the purple shades he swung,
Down the mountain, through the glen;
Towards the sound of fellow-men,
Even from the light that clung.

Dimly too, as cloud on cloud,
Came that silent flock of his:
Thronging whiteness, in a crowd,
After homing twos and threes;

With the longing memories
Of all white things dreamed and vowed.

Through the fragrances, alone,
By the sudden-silent brook,
From the open world unknown,
To the close of speech and book;
There to find the foreign look
In the faces of his own.

Sharing was beyond his skill;
Shyly yet, he made essay:
Sought to dip, and share, and fill
Heart's-desire, from day to day.
But their eyes, some foreign way,
Looked at him; and he was still.

Last, he reached his arms to sleep,
Where the Vision waited, dim,
Still beyond some deep-on-deep.

And the darkness folded him,
Eager heart and weary limb.
All day long, he kept the sheep.

HARVEST-MOON: 1914 by JOSEPHINE PRESTON PEAODY
Over the twilight field,
The overflowing field,
Over the glimmering field,
And bleeding furrows with their sodden yield
Of sheaves that still did writhe,
After the scythe;
The teeming field and darkly overstrewn
With all the garnered fulness of that noon
Two looked upon each other.
One was a Woman men called their mother;
And one, the Harvest-Moon.

And one, the Harvest-Moon,
Who stood, who gazed
On those unquiet gleanings where they bled;
Till the lone Woman said:
"But we were crazed...
We should laugh now together, I and you,
We two.
You, for your dreaming it was worth
A star's while to look on and light the Earth;
And I, forever telling to my mind,
Glory it was, and gladness, to give birth
To humankind!
Yes, I, that ever thought it not amiss
To give the breath to men,
For men to slay again:
Lording it over anguish but to give
My life that men might live

For this.
You will be laughing now, remembering
I called you once Dead World, and barren thing,

Yes, so we named you then,
You, far more wise
Than to give life to men."

Over the field, that there
Gave back the skies
A shattered upward stare
From blank white eyes,
Striving awhile, through many a bleeding dune
Of throbbing clay, but dumb and quiet soon,
She looked; and went her way
The Harvest-Moon.

HORSEMAN SPRINGING FROM THE DARK: A DREAM by LILLA CABOT PERRY

"Horseman, springing from the dark,
Horseman, flying wild and free,
Tell me what shall be thy road
Whither speedest far from me?"

"From the dark into the light,
From the small unto the great,
From the valleys dark I ride
O'er the hills to conquer fate!"

"Take me with thee, horseman mine!
Let me madly rode with thee!"
As he turned I met his eyes,
My own soul looked back at me!

THREE QUATRAINS by LILLA CABOT PERRY

THE CUP
She said, "Lift high the cup!"
Of her arm's weariness she gave no sign,
But, smiling, raised it up
That none might see or guess it held no wine.

FORGIVE ME NOT!
Forgive me not! Hate me and I shall know
Some of Love's fire still burns within your breast!
Forgiveness finds its home in hearts at rest,
On dead volcanoes only lies the snow.

THE ROSE
One deep red rose I dropped into his grave,
So small a thing to give so great a friend!
Yet well he knew it was my heart I gave
And must fare on without it to the end,

A VALENTINE, UNSENT by MARGARET PERRY

Stay, flaming rose, 'twould grieve her heart
To see you fade away,
Unloved, unwelcome and apart
From every joy to-day.

Once long ago your tale was new,
Days distant yet so dear;
Why say her lover still is true,
When that is all her fear?

Why thus recall another's pain,
Her tender heart to fret?
Best let her think he loves again,
Who never can forget!

SHIPBUILDERS by ARTHUR STANWOOD PIE

The German people reared them
An idol made of wood;
And Hindenburg before them
Lifelike and stupid stood.

To clothe him all in iron
And thus his soul express,
With nails and spikes they covered
His wooden nakedness.

And when they, thus had clothed him
All in a suit of mail,
Still came they, wild-eyed, looking
For space to drive a nail.
Whenever Teuton airmen
Slay boys and girls at play,
Or U-boats, drowning babies,
Create a holiday.

Then, gathering round their statue,
A happy German throng
Drive nails into the idol
To make him still more strong.

Avenge the babes, shipbuilders,
That on the seas have died;
Avenge the little children
Murdered for Wilhelm's pride.
Come, gather at the shipyards,
And let your hammers ring,
For more than ships and cargoes
Waits on your fashioning.

Come, gather at the shipyards;
With every bolt you drive
Bethink you `tis the Kaiser

Whose brutish head you rive.

Come, gather at the shipyards,
And swing with might and main;
`Tis Tirpitz and the Crown Prince
That you to-day have slain.

Come, gather at the shipyards,
And heat the metal hot,
For it is Bethmann Hollweg
You're boiling in the pot.

Come, gather at the shipyards,
And when the day is done,
You've spent it in driving spikes,
In Hindernburg the Hun.

Come, gather at the shipyards,
And toil with healthy hate,
For only you can save the world,
The Hun is at the gate.

UNFADING PICTURES by LOUELLA C. POOLE

("The air from the sea came blowing in again, mixed with the perfume of the flowers....
The old-fashioned furniture brightly rubbed and polished, my aunt's inviolable chair and
table by the round green fan in the bow-window, the drugget-covered carpet, the cat,
the kettle-holder, the two canaries, the old china ... and, wonderfully out of keeping with
the rest, my dusty self upon the sofa, taking note of everything."
-"David Copperfield," Chapter XIII.)

How many are the scenes he limned,
With artist strokes, clear-cut and free
Our Dickens; time shall not efface
Their charm, and they will ever grace
The halls of memory.

Oft and again we turn to them,
To contemplate in pleased review;
And like some picture on the screen
Comes now to mind a favorite scene
His master-pencil drew:

Upon a sofa, stretched in sleep,
I see a small lad, spent and worn,
And by the window, stern and grim,
A silent figure watching him,
So dusty, ragged, torn.

Ah, now she rises from behind
The round green fan beside her chair;
"Poor fellow!" croons-and pity lends
Her voice new softness-and she bends
And brushes back his hair.

Then in his sleep he softly stirs.
Was that a dream, these murmured words?
He wakes! There by the casement sat
Miss Trotwood still; close by, her cat
And her canary birds.

The peaceful calm of that quaint room,
Its marks of comfort everywhere
Old china and mahogany
And blowing in, fresh from the sea,
The perfume-laden air.

Poor little pilgrim so bereft,
So weary at his journey's end!
What joy must then have filled his soul
To reach at last such happy goal
To find, oh, such a friend!...

And then night came, and from his bed
He saw the sea, moonlit and bright,
And dreamed there came, to bless her son,
His mother, with her little one,
Adown that path of light.

Ah, greater blessing I'd not crave,
When my life's pilgrimage is o'er,
Than such repose, content, and love;
Some shining path that leads above
To dear ones gone before!

WITH WAVES AND WINGS by CHARLOTTE PORTER
Waves and Wings and Growing Things!
As through the gladden sight ye flow
And flit and glow,
Ye win me so
In soul to go,
I too am waves, I too am wings,
And kindred motion in me springs.

With thee I pass, glad growing grass!
I climb the air with lissome mien;
Unsheathing keen
The vivid sheen
Of springing green,
I thrill the crude, exalt the crass
Fine-flex'd and fluent from Earth's mass.

And impulse craves with thee, Sea Waves!
To make all mutable the floor
Of Earth's firm shore,
With flashing pour
Whose brimming o'er
Impassion'd motion loves and laves
And livens sombre slumbering caves.

Then soaring where the wild birds fare,
My song would sweep the windy lyre
Of Heaven's choir,
Pulsing desire
For starry fire,
Abashing chilling vagues of air
With throbbing of warm breasts that dare!

BLUEBERRIES by FRANK PRENTICE RAND
Upon the hills of Garlingtown
Beneath the summer sky,
In many pleasant pastures
On sunny slopes and high,
Their skins abloom with dusty blue,
Asleep, the berries lie.

And all the lads of Garlingtown,
And all the lasses too,
Still climb the tranquil hillsides,
A merry, barefoot crew;
Still homeward plod with unfilled pails
And mouths of berry blue.

And all the birds of Garlingtown,
When flocking back to nest,
Remember well the patches
Where berries are the best;
They pick the ripest ones at dawn
And leave the lads the rest.

Upon the hills of Garlingtown
When berry-time was o'er,
I looked into the sunset,
And saw an open door,
And from the hills of Garlingtown
I went, and came no more.

NOCTURNE by WILLIAM ROSCOE THAYER
Night of infinite power and infinite silence and space,
From you may mortals infer, if ever, the scope divine!
The jealous sun conceals all but his arrogant face,
You bid the Milky Way and a million suns to shine.

Each star to numberless planets gives light and motion and heat,
But you enmantle them all, the nearest and most remote;
And the lustres of all the suns are but spangles under your feet,
Mere bubbles and beads of noon, they circle and shine and float.

ENVOI by WILLIAM ROSCOE THAYER
I walked with poets in my youth,
Because the world they drew

Was beautiful and glorious
Beyond the world I knew.

The poets are my comrades still,
But dearer than in youth,
For now I know that they alone
Picture the world of truth.

THERE WHERE THE SEA by MARIE TUDOR
There where the sea enwrapt
A strip of land and wind-swept dune,
Where nature was quiescent in the glimmering
Noonday sun of early June,
The Placid sea lay shimmering
In a mist of blue,
From which the sky now drew
Its wealth of hue and colour;
One heard but the deep breathing of the ocean,
As it breathed along the shore in even motion.
Among the pines and listless of the scene,
Atthis and Alcaeus lay,
Within the heart of each a hunger
For the unknown gift of life.
Here from day to day
They met and dreamed away
The soft unfloding days of spring,
Now turning to the summer.

Aleaeus:
I am faint with all the fire
In my blood,
And I would plunge into the quiet blue
And lose all sense of time and you.

Atthis:
I, too, would plunge
And swim with you!

Doffing her robe, the maid stood in her beauty,
Calm and sure and unafraid,
The sinuous splendour of her limbs,
A silent symphony of curving line,
Which reached its final note
In breast and rounded throat.
He had not known that flesh could be so fair;
Each movement which she made
Wove o'er his sense a deeper spell,
Her beauty swept him like a flame
And caught him unaware.
She looked into his eyes, then dropping hers
Before that burning gaze,
Softly turned and crept with sunlit shoulders
Down among the boulders,
To the sea.
Secure within its covering depth

She called to him to follow.
She led him out along the tide,
With swift unerring stroke,
Nor paused till he was at her side.
With conquering arm
He seized her and from her brow
Tossed back the dripping locks, and sought her lips
Her eyes closed,
As all her body yielded to his kiss.
Then home he bore her to the shore,
Within his heart a song of triumph;
In hers, a new-born joy of womanhood.
So spring for them passed on to summer.

MARRIAGE by MARIE TUDOR
You, who have given me your name,
And with your laws have made me wife,
To share your failures and your fame,
Whose word has made me yours for life.

What proof have you that you hold me?
That in reality I'm one
With you, through all eternity?
What proof when all is said and done?

In spite of all the laws you've made,
I'm free. I am no part of you.
But wait-the last word is not said;
You're mine, for I'm myself and you.

All through my veins there flows your blood,
In you there is no part of me.
By virtue of my motherhood
Through me you live eternally.

Pity by HAROLD VINAL
Oh do not Pity me because I gave
My heart when lovely April with a gust,
Swept down the singing lanes with a cool wave;
And do not pity me because I thrust
Aside your love that once burned as a flame.
I was as thirsty as a windy flower
That bares its bosom to the summer shower
And to the unremembered winds that came.
Pity me most for moments yet to be,
In the far years, when some day I shall turn
Toward this strong path up to our little door
And find it barred to all my ecstasy.
No sound of your warm voice the winds have borne
Only the crying sea upon the shore.

A ROSE TO THE LIVING by NIXON WATERMAN

A rose to the living is more
Than sumptuous wreaths to the dead;
In filling love's infinite store,
A rose to the living is more,
If graciously given before
The hungering spirit is fled,
A rose to the living is more
Than sumptuous wreaths to the dead.

THE STORM by G. O. WARREN

She reached for sunset fires,
And lived with stars and the sea,
The mountains for her temple,
The storm for priest had she.

Together a libation
They poured to the God she knew,
Such wine as ageless heavens
And lonely wisdom brew.

Now she has done with worship,
For her all rites are the same;
Yet the storm keeps green forever
The moss upon her name.

WHERE THEY SLEEP by G. O. WARREN

The fog inrolling, dark and still
Lies deep upon the crowded dead
As flooding sea upon the sands,
And quenches starlight overhead.

Long have they slept. Their separate dust
Has mingled with a nameless mould.
Only the slower-crumbling stones
Still tell so much as may be told.

And now in shoreless fog adrift
Like some lone mariner gliding by,
I lean above the drowning graves
And wonder when I too shall lie

Where evermore the tides of night
And earth will hide my lonely rest;
And Time will bid my love forget
To read the stone upon my breast.

BEAUTY by G. O. WARREN

Not flesh alone am I, when I can be
So swiftly caught in Beauty's shimmering thread
Whose slender fibres, woven, held by me,

With their frail strength my following heart have led.

Yea, not all mortal, not all death my mind,
When, watching by lone twilight waters' brim
I tremblingly decipher, as they wind,
Her deathless hieroglyphs, though strange and dim.

So for this faith, when Thou my dust shalt bring
To dust, remember well, Great Alchemist,
Yearly to change my wintry earth to spring,
That I with Beauty still may keep my tryst.

COMRADES by GEORGE EDWARD WOODBERRY
Where are the friends that I knew in my
Maying,
In the days of my youth, in the first of my
roaming?
We were dear; we were leal; O, far we went
straying;
Now never a heart to my heart comes homing!
Where is he now, the dark boy slender
Who taught me bare-back, stirrup and reins?
I love him; he loved me; my beautiful, tender
Tamer of horses on grass-grown plains.

Where is he now whose eyes swam brighter,
Softer than love, in his turbulent charms;
Who taught me to strike, and to fall, dear fighter,
And gather me up in his boyhood arms;
Taught me the rifle, and with me went riding,
Suppled my limbs to the horseman's war;
Where is he now, for whom my heart's biding,
Biding, biding but he rides far!

O love that passes the love of woman!
Who that hath felt it shall ever forget
When the breath of life with a throb turns human,
And a lad's heart is to a lad's heart set?
Ever, forever, lover and rover
They shall cling, nor each from other shall part
Till the reign of the stars in the heavens be 'over,
And life is dust in each faithful heart.

They are dead, the American grasses under;
There is no one now who presses my side;
By the African chotts I am riding asunder,
And with great joy ride I the last great ride.
I am fey; I am fein of sudden dying;
Thousands of miles there is no one near;
And my heart, all the night it is crying, crying
In the bosoms of dead lads darling-dear.

Hearts of my music, them dark earth covers;
Comrades to die, and to die for, were they;
In the width of the world there were no such rovers

Back to back, breast to breast, it was ours to stay;
And the highest on earth was the vow that we cherished,
To spur forth from the crowd and come back never more,
And to ride in the track of great souls perished
Till the nests of the lark shall roof us o'er.

Yet lingers a horseman on Altai highlands,
Who hath joy of me, riding the Tartar glissade,
And one, far faring o'er orient islands
Whose blood yet glints with my blade's accolade;
North, west, east, I fling you my last hallooing,
Last love to the breasts where my own has bled;
Through the reach of the desert my soul leaps pursuing
My star where it rises a Star of the Dead.

THE FLIGHT by GEORGE EDWARD WOODBERRY

I

O wild Heart, track the land's perfume,
Beach-roses and moor-heather!
All fragrances of herb and bloom
Fail, out at sea, together.
O follow where aloft find room
Lark-song and eagle-feather!
All ecstasies of throat and plume
Melt, high on yon blue weather.

O leave on sky and ocean lost
The flight creation dareth;
Take wings of love, that mounts the most:
Find fame, that furthest fareth!
Thy flight, albeit amid her host
Thee, too, night star-like beareth,
Flying, thy breast on heaven's coast,
The infinite outweareth.

II

"Dead o'er us roll celestial fires;
Mute stand Earth's ancient beaches;
Old thoughts, old instincts, old desires,
The passing hour outreaches;
The soul creative never tires
Evokes, adores, beseeches;
And that heart most the god inspires
Whom most its wildness teaches.

"For I will course through falling years
And stars and cities burning;
And I will march through dying cheers
Past empires unreturning;
Ever the world flame reappears
Where mankind power is earning,
The nations' hopes, the people's tears,
One with the wild heart yearning.

Friend of my many years!
When the great silence falls, at last, on me,
Let me not leave, to pain and sadden thee,
A memory of tears,
But pleasant thoughts alone.
Of one who was thy friendship's honored guest
And drank the wine of consolation pressed
From sorrows of thy own.
I leave with thee a sense
Of hands upheld and trials rendered less,
The unselfish joy which is to helpfulness
Its own great recompense.
The knowledge that from thine,
As from the garments of the Master, stole
Calmness and strength, the virtue which makes whole
And heals without a sign.
Yea more, the assurance strong
That love, which fails of perfect utterance here,
Lives on to fill the heavenly atmosphere
With its immortal song.

Have ye heard of our hunting, o'er mountain and glen,
Through cane-brake and forest, — the hunting of men?
The lords of our land to this hunting have gone,
As the fox-hunter follows the sound of the horn;
Hark! the cheer and the hallo! the crack of the whip,
And the yell of the hound as he fastens his grip!
All blithe are our hunters, and noble their match,
Though hundreds are caught, there are millions to catch.
So speed to their hunting, o'er mountain and glen,
Through cane-brake and forest, — the hunting of men!
Gay luck to our hunters! how nobly they ride
In the glow of their zeal, and the strength of their pride!
The priest with his cassock flung back on the wind,
Just screening the politic statesman behind;
The saint and the sinner, with cursing and prayer,
The drunk and the sober, ride merrily there.
And woman, kind woman, wife, widow, and maid,
For the good of the hunted, is lending her aid:
Her foot's in the stirrup, her hand on the rein,
How blithely she rides to the hunting of men!
Oh, goodly and grand is our hunting to see,
In this 'land of the brave and this home of the free.'
Priest, warrior, and statesman, from Georgia to Maine,
All mounting the saddle, all grasping the rein;
Right merrily hunting the black man, whose sin
Is the curl of his hair and the hue of his skin!
Woe, now, to the hunted who turns him at bay!
Will our hunters be turned from their purpose and prey?
Will their hearts fail within them? their nerves tremble, when
All roughly they ride to the hunting of men?
Ho! alms for our hunters! all weary and faint,

Wax the curse of the sinner and prayer of the saint.
The horn is wound faintly, the echoes are still,
Over cane-brake and river, and forest and hill.
Haste, alms for our hunters! the hunted once more
Have turned from their flight with their backs to the shore:
What right have they here in the home of the white,
Shadowed o'er by our banner of Freedom and Right?
Ho! alms for the hunters! or never again
Will they ride in their pomp to the hunting of men!
Alms, alms for our hunters! why will ye delay,
When their pride and their glory are melting away?
The parson has turned; for, on charge of his own,
Who goeth a warfare, or hunting, alone?
The politic statesman looks back with a sigh,
There is doubt in his heart, there is fear in his eye.
Oh, haste, lest that doubting and fear shall prevail,
And the head of his steed take the place of the tail.
Oh, haste, ere he leave us! for who will ride then,
For pleasure or gain, to the hunting of men?

A MYSTERY OF JOHN GREENLEAF WHITTIER

The river hemmed with leaning trees
Wound through its meadows green;
A low, blue line of mountains showed
The open pines between.

One sharp, tall peak above them all
Clear into sunlight sprang
I saw the river of my dreams,
The mountains that I sang!

No clue of memory led me on,
But well the ways I knew;
A feeling of familiar things
With every footstep grew.

Not otherwise above its crag
Could lean the blasted pine;
Not otherwise the maple hold
Aloft its red ensign.

So up the long and shorn foot-hills
The mountain road should creep;
So, green and low, the meadow fold
Its red-haired kine asleep.

The river wound as it should wind;
Their place the mountains took;
The white torn fringes of their clouds
Wore no unwonted look.

Yet ne'er before that river's rim
Was pressed by feet of mine,
Never before mine eyes had crossed
That broken mountain line.

A presence, strange at once and known,
Walked with me as my guide;
The skirts of some forgotten life
Trailed noiseless at my side.

Was it a dim-remembered dream?
Or glimpse through ions old?
The secret which the mountains kept
The river never told.

But from the vision ere it passed
A tender hope I drew,
And, pleasant as a dawn of spring,
The thought within me grew,

That love would temper every change,
And soften all surprise,
And, misty with the dreams of earth,
The hills of Heaven arise.

Take our hands, James Russell Lowell,
Our hearts are all thy own;
To-day we bid thee welcome
Not for ourselves alone.

In the long years of thy absence
Some of us have grown old,
And some have passed the portals
Of the Mystery untold;

For the hands that cannot clasp thee,
For the voices that are dumb,
For each and all I bid thee
A grateful welcome home!

For Cedarcroft's sweet singer
To the nine-fold Muses dear;
For the Seer the winding Concord
Paused by his door to hear;

For him, our guide and Nestor,
Who the march of song began,
The white locks of his ninety years
Bared to thy winds, Cape Ann!

For him who, to the music
Her pines and hemlocks played,
Set the old and tender story
Of the lorn Acadian maid;

For him, whose voice for freedom
Swayed friend and foe at will,
Hushed is the tongue of silver,
The golden lips are still!

For her whose life of duty
At scoff and menace smiled,
Brave as the wife of Roland,
Yet gentle as a Child.

And for him the three-hilled city
Shall hold in memory long,
Those name is the hint and token
Of the pleasant Fields of Song!

For the old friends unforgotten,
For the young thou hast not known,
I speak their heart-warm greeting;
Come back and take thy own!

From England's royal farewells,
And honors fitly paid,
Come back, dear Russell Lowell,
To Elmwood's waiting shade!

Come home with all the garlands
That crown of right thy head.
I speak for comrades living,
I speak for comrades dead!

MIDNIGHT by JAMES RUSSELL LOWELL
The moon shines white and silent
On the mist, which, like a tide
Of some enchanted ocean,
O'er the wide marsh doth glide,
Spreading its ghost-like billows
Silently far and wide.

A vague and starry magic
Makes all things mysteries,
And lures the earth's dumb spirit
Up to the longing skies:
I seem to hear dim whispers,
And tremulous replies.

The fireflies o'er the meadow
In pulses come and go;
The elm-trees' heavy shadow
Weighs on the grass below;
And faintly from the distance
The dreaming cock doth crow.

All things look strange and mystic,
The very bushes swell
And take wild shapes and motions,
As if beneath a spell;
They seem not the same lilacs
From childhood known so well.

The snow of deepest silence

O'er everything doth fall,
So beautiful and quiet,
And yet so like a pall;
As if all life were ended,
And rest were come to all.

O wild and wondrous midnight,
There is a might in thee
To make the charmed body
Almost like spirit be,
And give it some faint glimpses
Of immortality!

A REQUIEM by JAMES RUSSELL LOWELL

Ay, pale and silent maiden,
Cold as thou liest there,
Thine was the sunniest nature
That ever drew the air;
The wildest and most wayward,
And yet so gently kind,
Thou seemedst but to body
A breath of summer wind.

Into the eternal shadow
That girds our life around,
Into the infinite silence
Wherewith Death's shore is bound,
Thou hast gone forth, beloved!
And I were mean to weep,
That thou hast left Life's shallows
And dost possess the Deep.

Thou liest low and silent,
Thy heart is cold and still.
Thine eyes are shut forever,
And Death hath had his will;
He loved and would have taken;
I loved and would have kept.
We strove,-and he was stronger,
And I have never wept.

Let him possess thy body,
Thy soul is still with me,
More sunny and more gladsome
Than it was wont to be:
Thy body was a fetter
That bound me to the flesh,
Thank God that it is broken,
And now I live afresh!

Now I can see thee clearly;
The dusky cloud of clay,
That hid thy starry spirit,
Is rent and blown away:
To earth I give thy body,

Thy spirit to the sky,
I saw its bright wings growing,
And knew that thou must fly.

Now I can love thee truly,
For nothing comes between
The senses and the spirit,
The seen and the unseen;
Lifts the eternal shadow,
The silence bursts apart,
And the soul's boundless future
Is present in my heart.

STANZAS ON FREEDOM by JAMES RUSSELL LOWELL
Men! whose boast it is that ye
Come of fathers brave and free,
If there breathe on earth a slave,
Are ye truly free and brave?
If ye do not feel the chain,
When it works a brother's pain,
Are ye not base slaves indeed,
Slaves unworthy to be freed?

Women! who shall one day bear
Sons to breathe New England air,
If ye hear, without a blush,
Deeds to make the roused blood rush
Like red lava through your veins,
For your sisters now in chains,-
Answer! are ye fit to be
Mothers of the brave and free?

Is true Freedom but to break
Fetters for our own dear sake,
And, with leathern hearts, forget
That we owe mankind a debt?
No! true freedom is to share
All the chains our brothers wear
And, with heart and hand, to be
Earnest to make others free!

They are slaves who fear to speak
For the fallen and the weak;
They are slaves who will not choose
Hatred, scoffing, and abuse,
Rather than in silence shrink
From the truth they needs must think;
They are slaves who dare not be
In the right with two or three.